# DO-IT-YOURSELF
# Math Stories

**20 Math Adventures Ready to Personalize: Addition • Subtraction Multiplication • Division • Time • Problem Solving • and More!**

## by Allyne Brumbaugh

SCHOLASTIC
PROFESSIONAL BOOKS

New York ■ Toronto ■ London ■ Auckland ■ Sydney

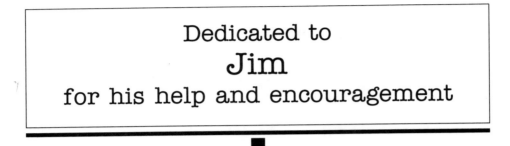

Dedicated to
## Jim
for his help and encouragement

Designed by Nancy Metcalf
Production by Intergraphics
Cover design by Vincent Ceci
Cover illustration by Mona Mark
Illustrations by Terri Chicko, Joe Chicko, Anna Cota-Robles

ISBN 0-590-49155-5

# Contents

# Note to Teachers

I began writing these stories several years ago in an attempt to motivate a group of children who were not very interested in math. The first story ("The House on Haunted Hill") was such a success that I followed it with "Visitors from Space." The children couldn't wait for more "stories about us."

I've used the stories ever since. They have come along with me from the urban school where I originally taught to the suburban school I currently teach in. They've worked equally well in both schools. Children like to read about themselves and their friends—in these stories *they* are the stars! Each year the names of the children in the stories change. The numbers also change, to fit the circumstances and the math level of the class.

The book is divided into three sections. In the first two sections, computational operations are emphasized— addition and subtraction or multiplication and division. (Most of the multiplication and division problems can also be done as repeated addition or subtraction.) There is also a group of stories that deals with money and time problems.

Some of the questions are basic word problems. Others are more complex (i.e., they may use more than one operation or have more than one solution, or they can be solved using one or more strategies that are not immediately apparent, etc.). For these more complex problems, children will need to use problem-solving techniques such as finding patterns, making organized lists and tables, guessing and checking, drawing diagrams, and using logical reasoning. Answers (on pages 93–96) are given for these more involved problems and for those questions for which I have supplied the numbers.

Much mathematical discussion has been generated in my classes as children search for the necessary information, explain their reasoning, and defend their strategies.

I hope that you and your class have many exciting adventures with this book.

# How To Use This Book

There are several ways to use the stories, but I suggest that you personalize the first one and do it as a whole class activity. In this way you can model the kinds of strategies your students may use to solve the problems.

Fill in the blanks by printing or typing the names of your students, your name, geographical information, etc. Generally, any child's name can be used in any name space. However, if the word "child" is followed by a letter (Example: "child A"), then that particular name will be used again in the story whenever the same letter appears.

At the same time fill in the number spaces. Some will be based on the number of children in your class. Other numbers are left to your choosing based on the needs of your students. You may wish to focus on basic number facts or more advanced computation.

Next you will need to copy the personalized story and questions for each child.

Start by having the children read the story aloud or to themselves. Then go through each problem one by one, always asking questions like the following:

- What information do you need to solve this problem?
- How can you solve the problem?
- Do you agree/disagree with the method?
- Does your answer make sense?
- Is there any other way to solve this problem?

Emphasis should be placed on mathematical reasoning, the communication of mathematical ideas, and problem-solving strategies rather than strictly on correct answers. Calculators and manipulative materials should be readily available.

You may wish to do the second story as a whole class activity as well, but this time copy and distribute the stories *before* the blanks are filled in. Have the children work with you to fill in the name and number spaces. Then go on and solve the problems.

By the third story the children should be experienced enough to work on their own. Divide the class into cooperative groups. Each group will fill in the blanks with names and numbers of their own choosing. They should then continue to work cooperatively to solve the problems.

# Extension and Alternative Activities

1. Give each cooperative group a different story to personalize. These stories can then be copied and the problems solved by the entire class.

2. Use just the story. Have the children write the questions (individually, in pairs, or in groups). Then copy and distribute the questions to the class.

3. Have the children write their own class story (or a continuation of one of these stories) and questions. Copy and distribute them to the entire class.

4. Try integrating some of these stories into units your class may be working on. "Planetarium Puzzle," "Visitors from Space," and "Future Park (Part 2)" might fit in with a unit on space. "Gerbil Trouble," "Missing at the Zoo," and "Adventure Beneath the Waves" would work well with units on animals. "Back to the Past" would be a perfect addition to a unit on dinosaurs, and what better time for "The House on Haunted Hill" than Halloween!

# The House on Haunted Hill

_____ took _____ class on a trip to Haunted Hill. There
(teacher)                              (his/her)

were _____ children in the class. _____ were girls and the rest were boys.
(#)                                  (#)

_____'s mother and _____'s mother went on the trip
(child)                              (child)

with the class.

The bus driver said to sit back and relax because it would be a long trip.

They would have to travel _____ miles in _____ and _____ miles
(#)                                          (name of town)                (#)

in _____ to get to Haunted Hill.
(name of town)

At last they reached Haunted Hill. The driver parked the bus at the

bottom of the hill and everyone walked up to the house. It was very spooky

looking. Some of the kids were scared. _____,
(children)

and _____ counted the windows. There were _____ windows.
(child)                                                     (#)

_____ of them were broken.
(#)

_____, _____, _____, and
(child A)                 (child B)                 (child C)

_____ went into the living room, where some ghosts were having
(child D)

a Halloween party. _____ and _____ counted _____
(child A)                (child B)                        (#)

boy ghosts. _____ and _____ counted _____ girl
(child C)                 (child D)                        (#)

ghosts. One of the ghosts said, "Won't you join us?" The children ran out

very quickly.

_____, _____, _____, and
(child E)                 (child F)                 (child G)

_____ climbed up _____ flights of stairs to the attic. Each flight
(child H)                         (#)

had _____ steps—all of which creaked. When the children saw the bats in the
(#)

attic, they all screamed. _____ screamed _____ times,
(child E)      (#)

_____ screamed twice, _____ screamed _____ times,
(child F)      (child G)      (#)

and _____ screamed once.
(child H)

_____, _____, _____, and
(child I)      (child J)      (child K)

_____ found the kitchen, where they saw _____ green goblins.
(child L)      (#)

_____ of the goblins were stirring a strange-looking brew. The others
(#)

were pouring the brew into cups for the ghosts' Halloween party.

_____, _____, and _____ wanted to taste
(child J)      (child K)      (child L)

the brew. _____ said they'd better not.
(child I)

_____, and _____
(children)      (child)

counted the number of rooms in the house. There were _____ rooms. _____
(#)      (#)

of them were locked. They were all very dusty. Each of the children sneezed

_____ times.
(#)

    Finally the bus driver said it was time to leave. When they got on the bus

_____ of the children said they had fun. _____
(#)      (teacher)

and the bus driver agreed. No one else liked the trip.

    Some people fell asleep on the way back to school (not the bus driver—

thank goodness). Nobody had a nightmare except _____ and
(child)

_____'s mother.
(child)

Name _____

# Now Try These...

How many. . .

**1.** of the children were boys? _____

**2.** people were on the bus? _____

**3.** miles away was the haunted house? _____

**4.** windows were unbroken? _____

**5.** steps were there to the attic?

_____

**6.** screams were heard? _____

**7.** doors were not locked? _____

**8.** people didn't like the trip? _____

Write a paragraph explaining how you solved this problem.

**9.** The bus driver found a secret staircase that had 10 slippery, slimy steps. It took the driver 1 minute to climb 3 steps, but each time he climbed up 3 steps, he slipped back 2. How long did it take him to reach the top step?

_____

**10.** One of the goblins was very clumsy. He broke 2 cups on Monday, 3 cups on Tuesday, 5 cups on Wednesday, 8 cups on Thursday, and 12 cups on Friday. If this pattern continues, how many cups will he break on Saturday?

_____

**11.** The answer is 8 ghosts. Think of a question that has this answer.

**10**

Name _____

**12.** It was a long bus ride home. Some children fell asleep. The teacher gave out copies of the magic X puzzle to keep the rest of the kids busy and was surprised when four children figured it out by the time they got back to school.

Try it yourself! Use the numbers 1 to 9 so that each of the two diagonals equals 26. The four corners of the X have to equal 26 as well.

**Make it easier!** Cut out nine squares of paper with the numbers 1 to 9 on them. Use these to try different arrangements on the X.

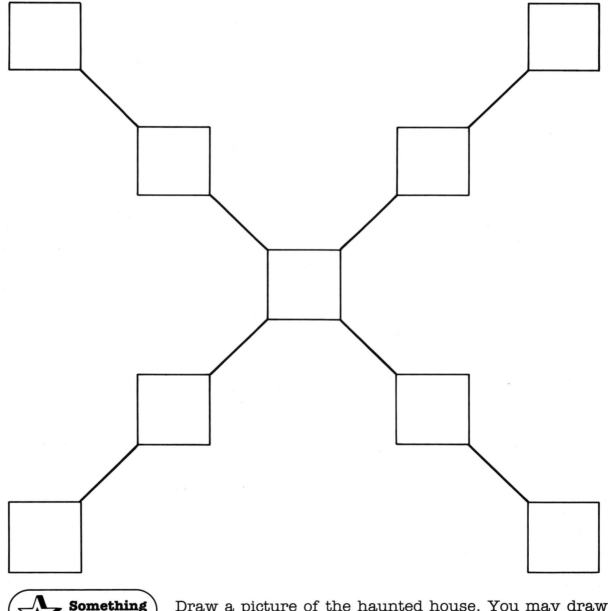

★ **Something Special**

Draw a picture of the haunted house. You may draw the outside, the inside, or both.

# Back to the Past (Part 1)

_____ was talking to _____ and _____,
(child A)                                          (child)                              (child)

but _____ spoke loudly enough for the whole class to hear. "My aunt has
(he/she)

invented a time machine. It can take you to any place and any time you

want to go."

There was a stunned silence. "I don't believe it!" yelled _____
(child)

and _____ in unison.
(child)

_____ asked, "Did she test it yet?"
(child)

"No," answered _____. "She's going to test it tomorrow, and
(child A)

she said we could all come and watch."

_____ said that whoever brought in a note from home
(teacher)

could go to _____'s aunt's laboratory to see the experiment.
(child A)

The next day everyone met at school. _____, _____,
(child)                              (child)

_____, _____, and _____ were so excited
(child)                        (child)                       (child)

they ran all the way. All _____ children had remembered to bring notes.
(#)

They walked to _____'s house together. _____ aunt's laboratory
(child A)                              (His/Her)

was in the basement. _____ said, "This is my Aunt _____."
(child A)                                            (name B)

Aunt _____ said, "At 9:30 this morning I will step into my
(name B)

time machine and go back 30 years in time."

The children smiled politely, but no one except _____ really
(child A)

believed her. Then Aunt _____ invited everyone into the time
(name B)

machine. It was pretty crowded with _____ children, _____, and
(#)                          (teacher)

**12**

Aunt _____. _____ accidently stepped on
        (name B)              (child)

_____'s foot. _____ fell backward and hit a control panel. The
      (child)            (He/She)

door slammed shut! Everyone started moving around. _____ fell
                                                          (child)

against the control lever and pulled it all the way down. "Oh no!" yelled

Aunt _____. "We're going back to the past!!!"
        (name B)

The time machine vibrated for 2 minutes. Then it was still. "Where are

we?" yelled _____ and _____ together.
                 (child)            (child)

"You mean *when* are we," said _____.
                                     (child)

"We must be back in the days of the dinosaurs," said _____
                                                            (child)

and _____ at the same time.
        (child)

"How do you know?" _____ asked.
                          (child)

"Just look out the window," _____ said.
                                   (child)

Everyone looked out the window. They saw _____ triceratops, _____
                                             (#)                    (#)

ankylosauruses, and _____ iguanodons looking at the time machine. From
                      (#)

another window _____, and
                                (children)

_____ saw _____ more triceratops.
      (child)          (#)

_____, and _____
                (children)                            (child)

were scared, but they wanted to get out of the time machine. It was getting

too hot and stuffy. They tried the door. It opened!

_____, and _____ led
                (children)                            (child)

the way. Finally everyone was out of the time machine. They looked around.

The dinosaurs seemed to have disappeared—for the moment!

Name _____

# Now Try These...

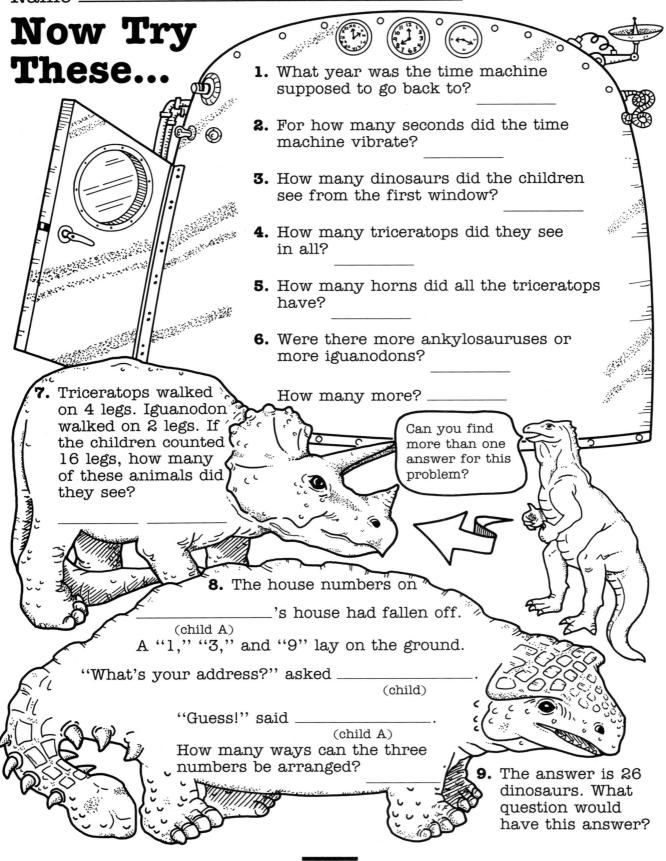

1. What year was the time machine supposed to go back to? _____

2. For how many seconds did the time machine vibrate? _____

3. How many dinosaurs did the children see from the first window? _____

4. How many triceratops did they see in all? _____

5. How many horns did all the triceratops have? _____

6. Were there more ankylosauruses or more iguanodons? _____

   How many more? _____

7. Triceratops walked on 4 legs. Iguanodon walked on 2 legs. If the children counted 16 legs, how many of these animals did they see?

   _____

Can you find more than one answer for this problem?

8. The house numbers on _____'s house had fallen off.
   (child A)
   A "1," "3," and "9" lay on the ground.

   "What's your address?" asked _____.
   (child)

   "Guess!" said _____.
   (child A)
   How many ways can the three numbers be arranged? _____

9. The answer is 26 dinosaurs. What question would have this answer?

Name _____

**10.** You can't spell "dinosaur" on a calculator, but you can spell "bee." Just enter the number 338. Now turn your calculator upside down and read the display: BEE.

Each numeral on the calculator looks like a letter of the alphabet when viewed upside down. Try it.

$$0 = O \quad 1 = i \quad 2 = Z \quad 3 = E \quad 4 = h$$
$$5 = S \quad 7 = L \quad 8 = B \quad (6 = g \text{ and } 9 = G)$$

**Try this problem.**

I had 543 baseball cards. I needed 394 more to have the most cards in my school. How many cards would make me the champ? (The correct answer is a part of your body.)

Did you get $543 + 394 = 937 = $ LEG?

These problems are not hard to make up. Follow these steps.

**Step 1** Choose a word using the calculator letters (Example: EEL).

**Step 2** See what numbers you need to enter on your calculator to get EEL (733).

**Step 3** Make up an equation that has an answer of 733 (Example: $245 + 488 = 733$ or $903 - 170 = 733$ or $1466 \div 2 = 733$).

**Step 4** Make up a word problem to fit the equation. (Example: I had 903 pennies in my bank yesterday. I have 170 today. How many did I spend?) Then make up a clue.

**Step 5** Give your problem to a friend to solve.

**Something Special**

If you had a time machine, would you go to the past or the future? Draw a picture of what you would see when you stepped out of the machine.

# Back to the Past (Part 2)

Aunt _____ said, "It will take me an hour to reset the time
(name B)

machine so we can get back to our own time."

_____ and _____ looked at each other and then at
(child)          (child)

_____. "Let's explore!"
(child)

"No way!" yelled _____ and _____.
(child)          (child)

_____ said they could vote on it. ____ of the ____
(teacher)                                (#)        (#)

children voted to explore. The rest voted to stay at the time machine. The

explorers won! _____, and
(children)

_____ cheered.
(child)

They walked up a hill, through thick bushes and trees. _____,
(child A)

_____, and _____ ran ahead and found a strange-
(child B)        (child C)

looking berry bush. It had red, yellow, and purple berries. _____
(child A)

picked ____ red berries. _____ picked ____ yellow berries.
(#)                       (child B)        (#)

_____ picked ____ purple berries. _____
(child C)          (#)                    (teacher)

wouldn't let them eat any. "They might be poisonous," ____ said.
(he/she)

When they reached the top of the hill, they looked down on a huge lake.

Several species of dinosaurs were in and around the lake.

_____, _____, and _____ counted
(child)       (child)          (child)

____ plateosauruses. _____ and _____ counted
(#)                   (child)          (child)

____ iguanodons. _____ pointed to the sky, where several
(#)               (child)

pterodactyls were flying overhead. _____, and
(children)

_____ counted them. Altogether the children counted ____ animals.
(child)                                                      (#)

They kept walking until they came to a cave. Most of the kids refused to go in. So _____ and _____ said they would take a look.
(child D)                    (child)

About three minutes later the two children came running out. "There's a whole bunch of eggs in there! We found 2 smaller caves and each one had _____ eggs."
(#)

"Do you think they are dinosaur eggs?" asked _____.
(child)

Everyone nodded.

"Let's leave before their mothers get back," said _____ in a
(child)

worried voice.

The class headed back to the time machine. They went past the lake, down the hill, through the trees and bushes. Finally, they saw the time machine— and something else, too. A tyrannosaurus rex was standing next to the time machine. It was huge! The time machine was 12 feet high, and the tyrannosaurus rex was 6 feet taller.

They could see Aunt _____ inside the time machine. "Come
(name B)

on," said _____. "We'll have to sneak past it."
(child)

The tyrannosaurus rex didn't seem to notice them as they tiptoed past it. Once they were inside, Aunt _____ pulled the lever. The time
(name B)

machine began vibrating again.

Two minutes later they found themselves back in the basement again.

"What an adventure!" said _____.
(child)

"No one will ever believe us," said _____.
(child)

"Maybe they will," said _____ as _____ unzipped _____
(child D)                    (he/she)              (his/her)

jacket and took out a very large egg.

"Fantastic!" said Aunt _____. "Fantastic!"
(name B)

Name _____

# Now Try These...

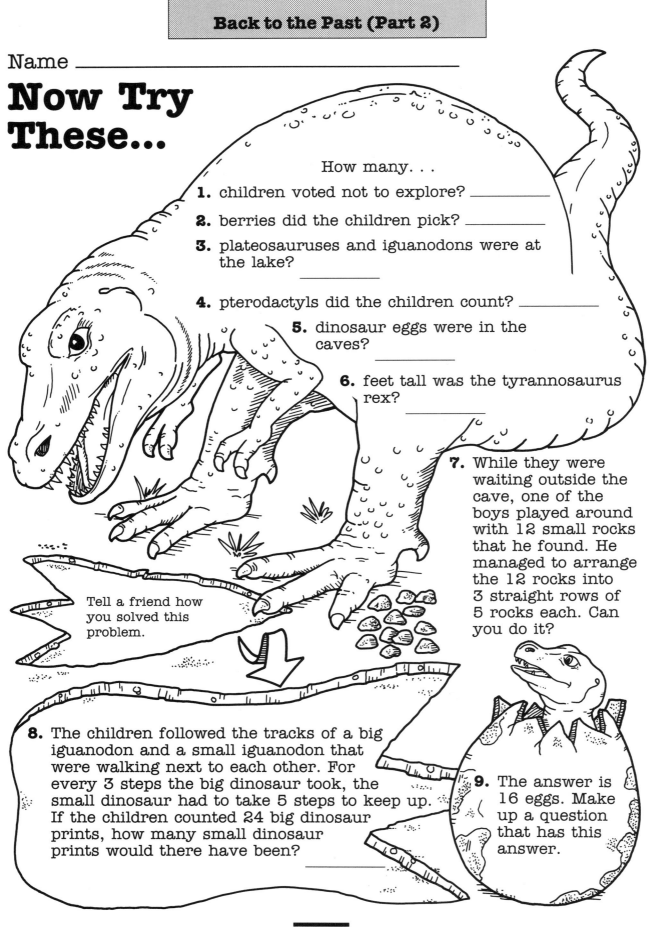

How many. . .

**1.** children voted not to explore? _____

**2.** berries did the children pick? _____

**3.** plateosauruses and iguanodons were at the lake? _____

**4.** pterodactyls did the children count? _____

**5.** dinosaur eggs were in the caves? _____

**6.** feet tall was the tyrannosaurus rex? _____

**7.** While they were waiting outside the cave, one of the boys played around with 12 small rocks that he found. He managed to arrange the 12 rocks into 3 straight rows of 5 rocks each. Can you do it?

Tell a friend how you solved this problem.

**8.** The children followed the tracks of a big iguanodon and a small iguanodon that were walking next to each other. For every 3 steps the big dinosaur took, the small dinosaur had to take 5 steps to keep up. If the children counted 24 big dinosaur prints, how many small dinosaur prints would there have been? _____

**9.** The answer is 16 eggs. Make up a question that has this answer.

Name _____

**10.** On their next trip the class would like to go back to see the Wright Brothers fly the first airplane. What year will they be traveling back to?

**Clue 1.** The year is after 1900.

**Clue 2.** The year is before 1920.

**Clue 3.** The sum of its digits is less than 17.

**Clue 4.** The sum of its digits is odd.

**Clue 5.** Its last two digits add up to more than 2.

**Clue 6.** The difference between the sum of its first two digits and last two digits is not 5.

**Clue 7.** Its first digit plus its third digit do not equal its last digit.

**Make it easier!** Use Clues #1 and #2 to help you make a list of the possible years.

The answer is _____

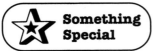
**Something Special**
Draw a picture of what hatched out of the dinosaur egg.

# Batter Up!

"It's about time we got here!" yelled _____ (child) as all _____ (#)
children got off the bus in front of _____ (name of baseball stadium) .

"We've probably already missed the 1st inning," said _____ (child) .

_____ (children) , and _____ (child) began
running up the ramp.

"Children, wait!" said _____ (teacher) . "We must stay together."

The children of Room \_\_\_\_\_ (#) had won this trip to see the

_____ (home team) play the _____ (visiting team) by collecting the

most cans for recycling. Their class had collected \_\_\_\_\_ (#) cans. The next

closest class had only collected \_\_\_\_\_ (#) .

_____ (children) , and _____ (child) led
the way to the bleachers. By the time the children got there, it was the top of

the 3rd inning.

"Oh no, we're losing," moaned _____ (child) .

"It's only 1 to 0," said _____ (child) .

"Let's just hurry up and get our seats!" exclaimed _____ (child) .

Because there were so many children they had to sit in four different

rows. _____ (children) , and _____ (child)
sat in the 1st row. _____ (children) , and

_____ (child) sat in the 2nd row. The rest of the children and

_____ (teacher) sat in the 3rd and 4th rows.

"I want peanuts!" shouted _____ (child) . "Me too!" said

_____ (child) . \_\_\_\_\_ (#) children wanted peanuts. \_\_\_\_\_ (#) wanted popcorn.

_____ children wanted ice cream. And the rest wanted hot dogs.
(#)

Neither team scored during the next four innings.

"This is boring!" said _____.
(child)

"I don't even like baseball," said _____.
(child)

"Let's go home!" yelled _____ and _____ at the
(child) (child)
same time.

"Sorry," said _____. "We're staying until the end of the
(teacher)
game."

_____ and _____ were glad.
(child) (child)

Then things started to get more exciting. The _____
(visiting team)
scored _____ runs in the 7th inning, _____ runs in the 8th inning, and
(#) (#)
_____ runs in the 9th inning.
(#)

The _____ scored _____ runs in the 7th inning, _____
(home team) (#) (#)
runs in the 8th inning, and _____ runs in the 9th inning.
(#)

The game was over! The _____ had won.
(home/visiting team)

"O.K.," said _____. "Now we can go home."
(teacher)

The children cheered, especially those who had rooted for the winning

team.

Name _____

# Now Try These...

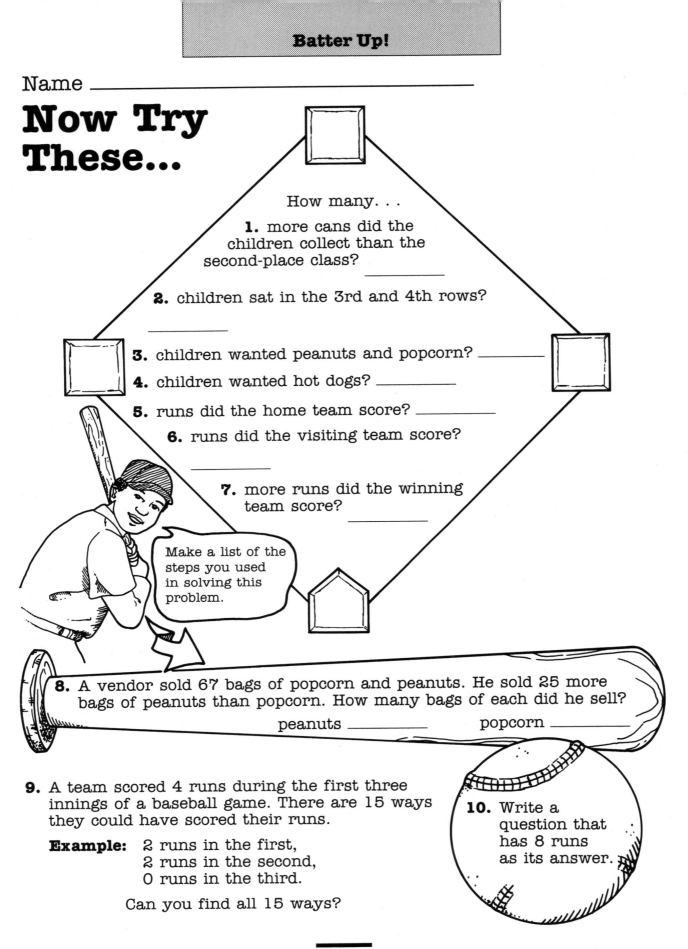

How many...

**1.** more cans did the children collect than the second-place class? _____

**2.** children sat in the 3rd and 4th rows?

_____

**3.** children wanted peanuts and popcorn? _____

**4.** children wanted hot dogs? _____

**5.** runs did the home team score? _____

**6.** runs did the visiting team score?

_____

**7.** more runs did the winning team score?

_____

Make a list of the steps you used in solving this problem.

**8.** A vendor sold 67 bags of popcorn and peanuts. He sold 25 more bags of peanuts than popcorn. How many bags of each did he sell?

peanuts _____     popcorn _____

**9.** A team scored 4 runs during the first three innings of a baseball game. There are 15 ways they could have scored their runs.

**Example:**   2 runs in the first,
2 runs in the second,
0 runs in the third.

Can you find all 15 ways?

**10.** Write a question that has 8 runs as its answer.

Name _____

**11.** Here is the American League scoreboard for one day in June. Use the clues and the numbers in the ball to fill in the missing scores. One is done as an example. (The winning team of each pair is the one on top.)

| TEAM | RUNS SCORED |
|---|---|
| ANGELS | 10 |
| RANGERS | 8 |
| RED SOX | |
| ORIOLES | |
| TIGERS | |
| INDIANS | |
| BREWERS | |
| YANKEES | |
| MARINERS | |
| BLUE JAYS | |
| WHITE SOX | |
| TWINS | |
| ROYALS | |
| A'S | |

**CLUES**

**a.** Angels and Rangers scored a total of 18 runs. There is a difference of 2 runs.

**b.** Red Sox and Orioles scored a total of 12 runs. There is a difference of 6 runs.

**c.** Tigers and Indians scored a total of 8 runs. There is a difference of 6 runs.

**d.** Brewers and Yankees scored a total of 7 runs. There is a difference of 3 runs.

**e.** Mariners and Blue Jays scored a total of 4 runs. There is a difference of 2 runs.

**f.** White Sox and Twins scored a total of 6 runs. There is a difference of 2 runs.

**g.** Royals and A's scored a total of 6 runs. There is a difference of 4 runs.

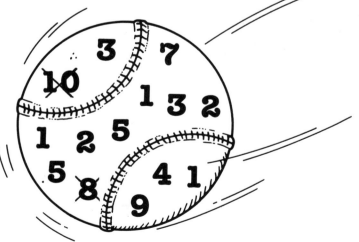

 **Something Special**
Make up a baseball card for an imaginary player. Use a real baseball card as a model for the information you'll need.

# Treasure Hunt

It started out as a normal Wednesday morning, but then

_____ made an unusual announcement. "Children, we're
(teacher)

going on a treasure hunt!"

_____, and _____
(children)                                        (child)

immediately looked up with interest. _____ and _____
(child)                              (child)

looked at each other and groaned. _____'s ideas usually
(teacher)

meant work.

"All you have to do is follow the clues and they will lead you to the

treasure," continued _____.
(teacher)

"Is there really a treasure?" asked _____.
(child)

"Yes, there really is a treasure, but I won't tell you what it is. Now here

are the clues. Good luck."

"O.K. What's the first clue?" asked _____.
(child)

"I'll read it," said _____. "It says, 'Start at the big oak tree.
(child)

Go north the number of meters equaled by: the legs on a spider, plus the legs

on a grasshopper, plus the legs on a peccary.'"

"What's a peccary?" asked _____.
(child)

_____, and _____
(children)                                        (child A)

ran to look up the word in the dictionary. "O.K. I've got it," said

_____. "Let's add up all those legs."
(child A)

"What's clue number two?" asked _____.
(child)

_____ and _____ read the clue together. "'Go east
(child)                (child)

the number of meters equaled by: the zeroes in a trillion, plus the hours in a day.'" Everyone was silent as the children tried to figure out how many

zeroes there were in a trillion.

"O.K. I've got it," said _____.
                                 (child)

"The third clue says, 'Go south the number of meters equal to: the nickels

in 2 dollars, take away the stripes on the American flag.'" _____
                                                                    (child)

went to count the stripes on the flag.

"O.K. I've got it," said _____.
                                 (child)

"Here's the last clue," said _____. "'Go east again, the
                                    (child)

number of meters equal to: the eggs in 2 dozen, plus the years in half a

century, take away the minutes in an hour."

"O.K. I've got it," said _____.
                                 (child)

The children took their meter sticks and went outside. They carefully

measured out the distances. The last clue led them to a bench. There, behind

the bench, was a small chest.

"Open it!" said _____. _____ and
                       (child)            (child)

_____ opened it. There was a loud gasp as the children looked
        (child)

down at a chest full of gold coins.

"It's impossible!" said _____.
                                (child)

"It's chocolate!" said _____.
                               (child)

"Delicious!" said all the kids.

Name _____

# Now Try These...

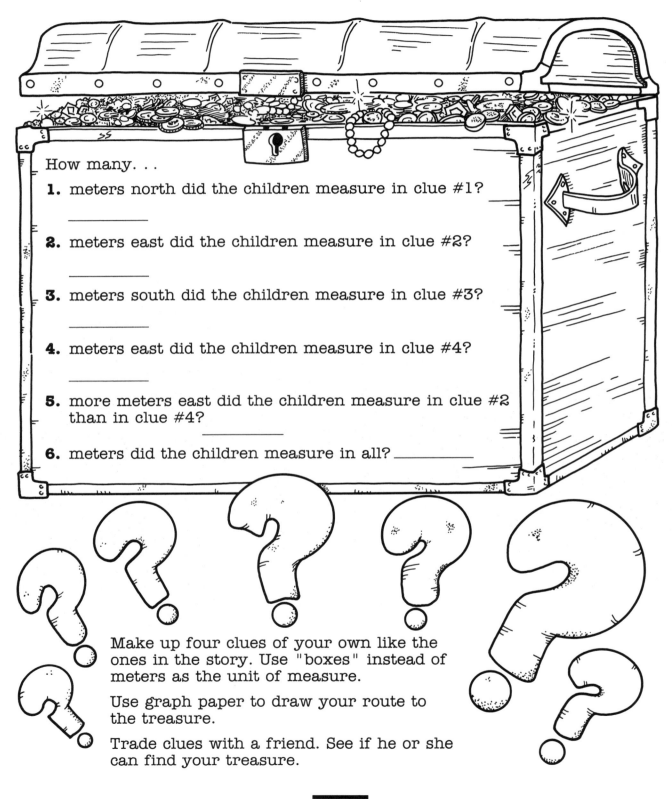

How many. . .

**1.** meters north did the children measure in clue #1?

_____

**2.** meters east did the children measure in clue #2?

_____

**3.** meters south did the children measure in clue #3?

_____

**4.** meters east did the children measure in clue #4?

_____

**5.** more meters east did the children measure in clue #2 than in clue #4?

_____

**6.** meters did the children measure in all? _____

Make up four clues of your own like the ones in the story. Use "boxes" instead of meters as the unit of measure.

Use graph paper to draw your route to the treasure.

Trade clues with a friend. See if he or she can find your treasure.

Name _____

Write your clues here:

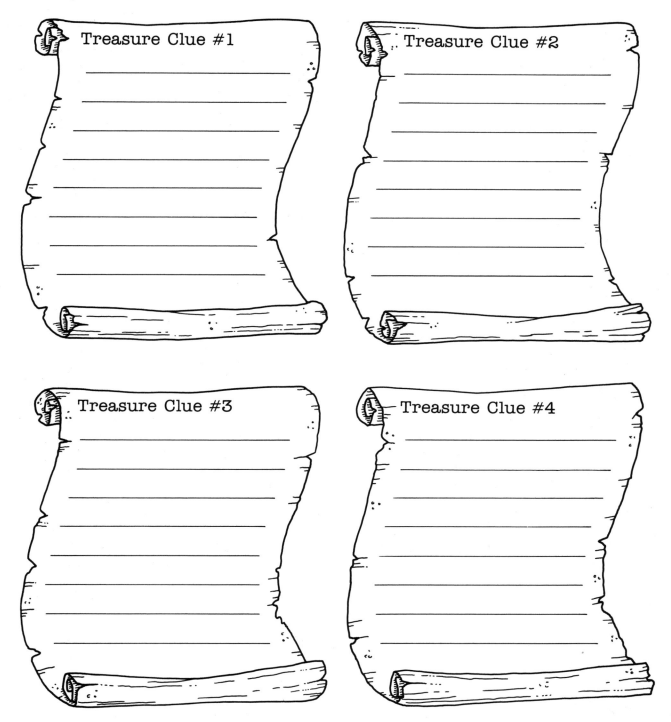

Treasure Clue #1

Treasure Clue #2

Treasure Clue #3

Treasure Clue #4

**Something Special**

What would *you* like to find in a treasure chest?
Draw it.

# Lost in the Woods

No schoolwork today! _____ (name of school) was on its yearly picnic

to _____ (name of park). Every class in the school was there. The

_____ (#) children of Room _____ (#) had managed to consume _____ (#) hamburgers

and _____ (#) hot dogs as well as tons of potato chips and watermelon. Now

some of them were eating chocolate bars as well.

Before lunch there had been games. _____ (child), _____ (child),

and _____ (child) had won a relay race. _____ (child) and

_____ (child) had come in second in the sack race. Now the kids were

ready for the hike through the woods that _____ (teacher) had

promised them.

"But remember," said _____ (teacher). "We have to be back here

at 2:00 P.M. or the bus will leave without us."

The woods were beautiful. _____ (child A) and _____ (child B)

collected rocks. _____ (child A) put _____ (#) rocks in each of _____ (his/her)

2 pockets. _____ (child B) put _____ (#) rocks into each of _____ (his/her)

2 pockets.

_____ (children), and _____ (child)

counted birds. Each of them counted _____ (#) birds.

_____ (children), and _____ (child)

pointed out different kinds of trees and flowers that they knew the names of.

They walked and walked. All of a sudden _____ (child C) said, "I don't

hear the other classes yelling or anything." _____ (child C) was right. The woods were absolutely quiet, except for the rustle of leaves and the call of birds.

Everyone looked at _____ (teacher). _____ (He/she) looked around. "I don't know where we are."

"We're lost!" yelled _____ (child) and _____ (child) together.

"I think we should go that way," said _____ (child), pointing right.

"I think we should go this way," said _____ (child), pointing left.

"We're going to stay right where we are until someone finds us," said

_____ (teacher).

They all sat down under a towering pine tree to wait. At 2:30 P.M.

_____ (children), and _____ (child) said they were hungry. There were 6 leftover chocolate bars. Each bar was divided into 6 little squares. _____ (child) broke up the bars so that each child could have a square.

At 3:00 P.M. _____ (children), and _____ (child) said they were thirsty, but there was no water.

At 3:15 P.M. _____ (child) and _____ (child) said they were scared. _____ (teacher) told them not to worry, but the kids thought the teacher looked pretty worried _____ (himself/herself).

Finally, at 3:30 P.M., they heard voices calling their names.

_____ (children), and _____ (child) started yelling, "Here we are!" They were found!

Back at the bus, _____ (child) said, "Next year, I'm bringing a compass!"

"Yeah," said _____. "And a canteen too!"

**29**

Name _____

# Now Try These...

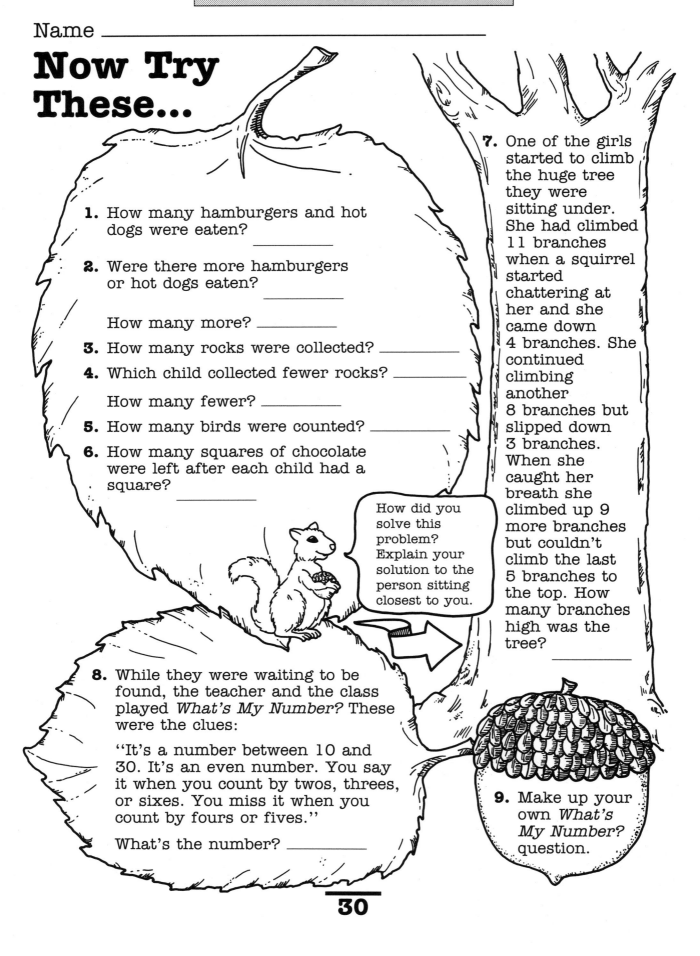

1. How many hamburgers and hot dogs were eaten? _____

2. Were there more hamburgers or hot dogs eaten? _____

   How many more? _____

3. How many rocks were collected? _____

4. Which child collected fewer rocks? _____

   How many fewer? _____

5. How many birds were counted? _____

6. How many squares of chocolate were left after each child had a square? _____

How did you solve this problem? Explain your solution to the person sitting closest to you.

7. One of the girls started to climb the huge tree they were sitting under. She had climbed 11 branches when a squirrel started chattering at her and she came down 4 branches. She continued climbing another 8 branches but slipped down 3 branches. When she caught her breath she climbed up 9 more branches but couldn't climb the last 5 branches to the top. How many branches high was the tree? _____

8. While they were waiting to be found, the teacher and the class played *What's My Number?* These were the clues:

   "It's a number between 10 and 30. It's an even number. You say it when you count by twos, threes, or sixes. You miss it when you count by fours or fives."

   What's the number? _____

9. Make up your own *What's My Number?* question.

Name _____

**10.** The candy bar in the story was made of 6 squares arranged like this:

How would a candy bar look if it were made of only 5 squares? There are 12 different ways to arrange 5 squares. They are called pentominoes.

Here are the rules:

**1.** At least one edge of each square must match up with an edge of another square.

like this:

not this:                    or this:

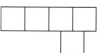
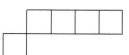

**2.** Each pentomino must be different. If you can turn it around or flip it over to make it look like another, then it is not different.

These are all the same:

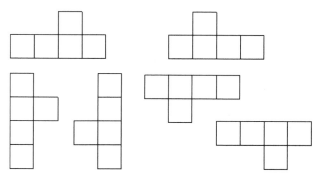

Can you find all 12 pentominoes? Use graph paper to draw them.

## TRY THIS

**1.** Mount your pentominoes on cardboard. Cut them out. Now, can you put them together like a jigsaw puzzle to form a

- 6 by 10 box rectangle?
- 5 by 12 box rectangle?
- 4 by 15 box rectangle?
- 3 by 20 box rectangle?

**2.** There are 35 hexominoes (made with 6 squares). Can you find them? (This is really hard. Work with a group.)

 **Something Special**   Invent a game that might have been played at the picnic. Explain the rules to your friends.

# Gerbil Trouble

_____ had brought a pair of gerbils to school. _____
(child)                                                              (teacher)
said they could keep the gerbils if the kids took care of them.

All went well for the first two weeks. _____,
                                                    (child)
_____, and _____ fed the gerbils.
      (child)                    (child)
_____, and _____
                (children)                              (child A)
cleaned the cage. Everyone played with the gerbils and learned about them.

Then, one morning, the children came into the classroom and found the

cage door open and the gerbils gone! _____ sadly admitted that
                                                   (child A)
_____ might have left the cage door open after cleaning it the day before.
(he/she)

And so the great gerbil hunt began. _____, _____,
                                                  (child)            (child)
and _____ looked under the radiators. They found _____ math
          (child)                                                        (#)
chips (_____ were blue and the rest were red), but no gerbils.
          (#)

_____, and _____ searched
                    (children)                                    (child)
the coat closet. They found _____ sweaters and _____ jackets, but no gerbils.
                                    (#)                    (#)

_____, and _____
                    (children)                                    (child)
went through the paper shelves. They found _____ packages of drawing
                                                        (#)
paper and _____ packages of writing paper, but no gerbils.
                (#)

_____, and _____
                    (children)                                    (child)
looked under the desks. They found _____ crayons (_____ were broken, the
                                            (#)                  (#)
rest were not), but no gerbils.

_____, and _____
                    (children)                                    (child)
checked the science center. They found _____ magnets and _____ magnifying
                                                (#)                    (#)
glasses, but no gerbils.

_____, and _____
(children) (child)

looked through all the desks. They found _____ pencils (_____ of them had
(#) (#)

erasers, the rest did not), but no gerbils.

Finally, _____ insisted that they stop looking and do
(teacher)

some school work. The gerbils, _____ said, would turn up. But they didn't.
(he/she)

All through the day the children watched and waited. At 3:00 P.M. it was

time to go home.

The children decided to leave some seeds and water in the middle of the

floor. They also left the cage there.

The kids were eager to return to school the next morning, but they were

disappointed to find—no gerbils. The food was gone, but so were the gerbils—

again!

They tried the same plan for the next two nights, but the same thing

happened. The gerbils ate the food, drank the water, and then went back to

their hiding place.

Then _____ had an idea. "The gerbils come out after we leave
(child B)

because it's dark and quiet in the room. Why don't we leave the lights on

when we go home today and not leave any food. Tomorrow morning, when

they're hungry, we'll make the room dark and put out food and water."

"We'll be real quiet," continued _____, "and when the gerbils
(child B)

come out, we'll grab them."

_____ agreed that _____'s idea might work.
(teacher) (child B)

Bright and early the next morning they tried it. Guess what—it _did_ work!

When the gerbils were back in the cage, everyone promised to be more

careful about closing the cage door. Next time!

Name _____

# Now Try These...

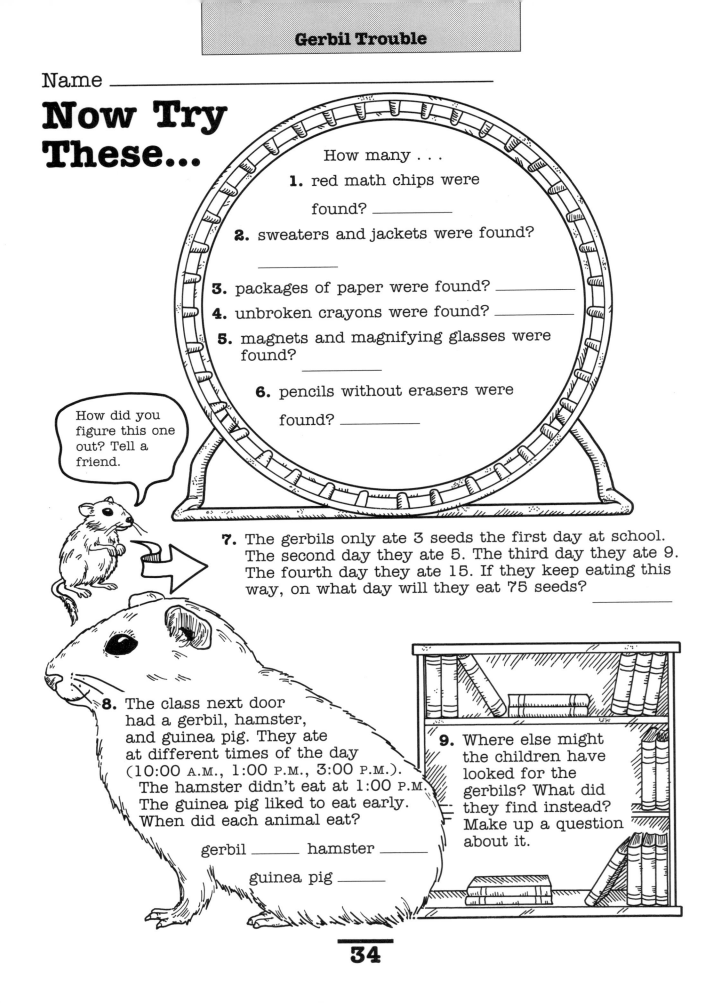

How many . . .

1. red math chips were found? _____

2. sweaters and jackets were found?

   _____

3. packages of paper were found? _____

4. unbroken crayons were found? _____

5. magnets and magnifying glasses were found? _____

6. pencils without erasers were found? _____

How did you figure this one out? Tell a friend.

7. The gerbils only ate 3 seeds the first day at school. The second day they ate 5. The third day they ate 9. The fourth day they ate 15. If they keep eating this way, on what day will they eat 75 seeds? _____

8. The class next door had a gerbil, hamster, and guinea pig. They ate at different times of the day (10:00 A.M., 1:00 P.M., 3:00 P.M.). The hamster didn't eat at 1:00 P.M. The guinea pig liked to eat early. When did each animal eat?

   gerbil _____ hamster _____

   guinea pig _____

9. Where else might the children have looked for the gerbils? What did they find instead? Make up a question about it.

**34**

Name _____

**Chart 1**

10. $\frac{A}{1}$ $\frac{B}{2}$ $\frac{C}{3}$ $\frac{D}{4}$ $\frac{E}{5}$ $\frac{F}{6}$ $\frac{G}{7}$ $\frac{H}{8}$ $\frac{I}{9}$ $\frac{J}{10}$ $\frac{K}{11}$ $\frac{L}{12}$ $\frac{M}{13}$

$\frac{N}{14}$ $\frac{O}{15}$ $\frac{P}{16}$ $\frac{Q}{17}$ $\frac{R}{18}$ $\frac{S}{19}$ $\frac{T}{20}$ $\frac{U}{21}$ $\frac{V}{22}$ $\frac{W}{23}$ $\frac{X}{24}$ $\frac{Y}{25}$ $\frac{Z}{26}$

Using the letter values above (Chart 1), the word "gerbil" is worth 53 points. However, if you reverse the point system, as shown below (Chart 2), then "gerbil" is worth 109 points.

**Chart 2**

$\frac{A}{26}$ $\frac{B}{25}$ $\frac{C}{24}$ $\frac{D}{23}$ $\frac{E}{22}$ $\frac{F}{21}$ $\frac{G}{20}$ $\frac{H}{19}$ $\frac{I}{18}$ $\frac{J}{17}$ $\frac{K}{16}$ $\frac{L}{15}$ $\frac{M}{14}$

$\frac{N}{13}$ $\frac{O}{12}$ $\frac{P}{11}$ $\frac{Q}{10}$ $\frac{R}{9}$ $\frac{S}{8}$ $\frac{T}{7}$ $\frac{U}{6}$ $\frac{V}{5}$ $\frac{W}{4}$ $\frac{X}{3}$ $\frac{Y}{2}$ $\frac{Z}{1}$

Listed below are nine other rodents. Predict whether Chart 1 or Chart 2 will give you the highest score for each word. Then see if you were right.

| Word | Prediction | Points using Chart 1 | Points using Chart 2 | Were you right? |
|---|---|---|---|---|
| rat | | | | |
| mouse | | | | |
| hamster | | | | |
| beaver | | | | |
| muskrat | | | | |
| squirrel | | | | |
| chipmunk | | | | |
| woodchuck | | | | |
| guinea pig | | | | |

 **Something Special**

Draw a picture of where the gerbils were hiding. Draw it from the gerbils' point of view.

# Planetarium Puzzle

"Hurry, hurry, hurry!" urged _____ (teacher) as the class ran
from the planetarium entrance to the Sky Theater. They reached the theater
just before the doors closed.

"Looks like you just made it," said a woman in a bright green dress as
she moved over to make room for the children.

The children looked up at the domed ceiling as the theater darkened. The
show was about constellations, which was just what the children were
studying in school.

_____ (children), and _____ (child)
counted the 7 stars of the Big Dipper.

_____ (children), and _____ (child)
found the 6 brightest stars of Cygnus the Swan.

_____ (children), and _____ (child)
recognized Pegasus the Winged Horse with its 16 stars.

_____ (children), and _____ (child)
looked for the 9 stars of Leo the Lion.

When the show was over the children stood up. All of a sudden they heard
the sound of breaking glass. A bunch of marbles had fallen out of
_____ (child A)'s pocket. When they hit the floor most of them broke.

"Don't touch them!" warned _____ (teacher). "Those pieces are
very sharp."

A guard came over carrying a broom and a dust pan. _____ (He/She) swept
up the glass and threw it in a trash can.

"How many marbles did you lose?" _____ asked.
                                         (child B)

"I don't know," answered _____. "I started out with _____
                                (child A)                          (#)

and I have _____ left."
             (#)

Later, _____, and _____
                       (children)                      (child)

weighed themselves on the Scales of Other Worlds. They were amazed at how

much they would weigh on the sun.

_____, and _____
               (children)                      (child)

learned some things about the planets. They found out that a day on Jupiter

is only 10 hours long, that it takes Pluto 248 years to orbit the sun, and a

lot of other facts.

Then it was time for lunch. _____ went to buy milk for
                                      (teacher)

all _____ children. _____ of them wanted plain milk. The rest asked for
      (#)             (#)

chocolate milk.

Just before they left the cafeteria the planetarium director came in with

the woman wearing the bright green dress.

"May I have your attention?" the director said. "This woman has lost a

valuable diamond from her ring. We've searched the whole planetarium, but

we can't find it. Has anyone seen it?"

_____ and _____ looked at each other.
      (child A)               (child B)

_____ stood up and told the director about the broken marbles.
      (child A)

"Maybe the diamond was on the floor and got swept up with the broken glass."

The director and the woman in bright green ran out to check. Sure

enough, they found the diamond in the trash. The planetarium director gave

the children a beautiful book about constellations for their classroom library.

All the children agreed that they'd like to come back soon for the next show.

Name _____

# Now Try These...

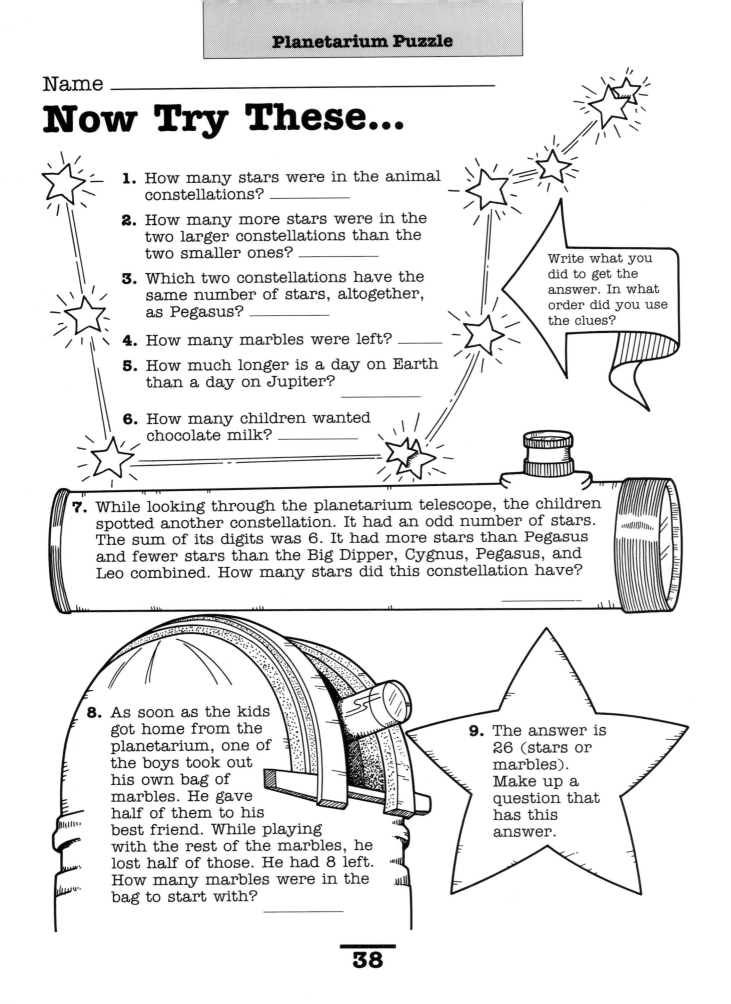

**1.** How many stars were in the animal constellations? _____

**2.** How many more stars were in the two larger constellations than the two smaller ones? _____

**3.** Which two constellations have the same number of stars, altogether, as Pegasus? _____

**4.** How many marbles were left? _____

**5.** How much longer is a day on Earth than a day on Jupiter? _____

**6.** How many children wanted chocolate milk? _____

Write what you did to get the answer. In what order did you use the clues?

**7.** While looking through the planetarium telescope, the children spotted another constellation. It had an odd number of stars. The sum of its digits was 6. It had more stars than Pegasus and fewer stars than the Big Dipper, Cygnus, Pegasus, and Leo combined. How many stars did this constellation have? _____

**8.** As soon as the kids got home from the planetarium, one of the boys took out his own bag of marbles. He gave half of them to his best friend. While playing with the rest of the marbles, he lost half of those. He had 8 left. How many marbles were in the bag to start with? _____

**9.** The answer is 26 (stars or marbles). Make up a question that has this answer.

Name _____

**10.** The children learned about moons at the planetarium. Our planet, Earth, has only 1 moon. Can you use the Moon Clues to help you find out how many moons the other planets have?

### MOON CLUES

**a.** Mercury's moons equal Pluto's moons take away Earth's moon.

**b.** Venus and Mercury have the same number of moons.

**c.** Mars has 1 more moon than Earth.

**d.** Adding the moons of Earth, Mars, and Pluto 4 times will equal Jupiter's moons.

**e.** Saturn has the most moons—2 more than the planet with the second-most moons.

**f.** The moons of Uranus equal Jupiter's moons take away Pluto's moons.

**g.** Neptune has half as many moons as Jupiter.

**h.** Pluto has 1 less moon than Mars.

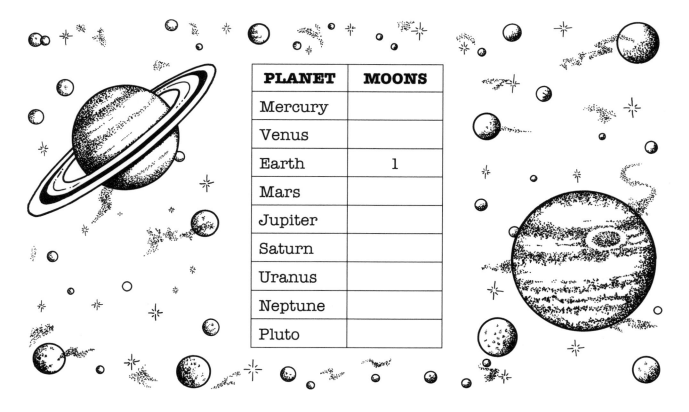

| PLANET | MOONS |
|---|---|
| Mercury | |
| Venus | |
| Earth | 1 |
| Mars | |
| Jupiter | |
| Saturn | |
| Uranus | |
| Neptune | |
| Pluto | |

 **Something Special** Draw and name your own constellation. Most constellations have legends that go along with them. Can you make up a story for your constellation?

# Visitors from Space

The _____ children of Room _____ were busy working when all of a
    (#)                     (#)

sudden they heard a strange noise coming from outside. _____
                                                  (child)

ran to the window. "Wow!" _____ said. "There's a spaceship landing on
                             (he/she)

_____."
(name of street A)

_____, and _____
           (children)                          (child)

wanted to go outside to see it, but _____ said it might be
                                   (teacher)

dangerous. So they had to look out the windows. There were _____ windows
                                             (#)

and _____ children watched from each one. _____ kids were afraid to look.
   (#)                                   (#)

_____, and _____
           (children)                          (child)

ran as fast as they could to the office to tell _____ and to
                                         (principal)

call the police.

The spaceship was very strange looking. It was shaped like a cube. There

were _____ windows on each face. Half of the windows had aliens looking out
    (#)

of them.

All of a sudden _____, and
                            (children)

_____ noticed something that was quite frightening.
   (child)

_____, and _____ were
           (children)                      (child A)

gone! They were so excited that they had run outside.

_____ was very worried. _____ sent _____
   (teacher)                       (He/She)          (child)

and _____ to get them. Then the children in the classroom saw
     (child)

_____ pointing down _____. _____ police cars
  (child A)                   (name of Street A)     (#)

were coming down the street. _____ police officers got out of each car. They
                           (#)

surrounded the spaceship.

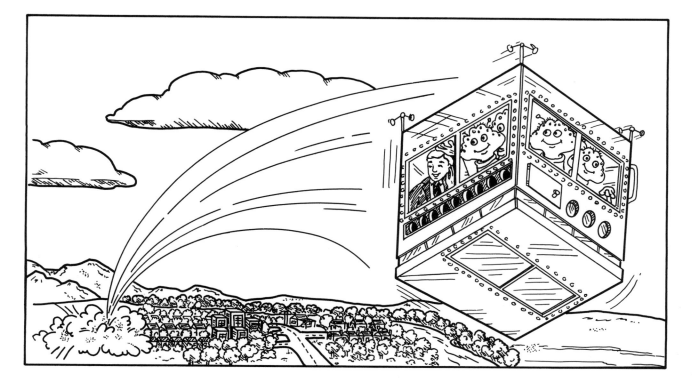

Finally the door of the spaceship opened. Two strange-looking creatures walked out. Each of the alien creatures had _____ heads. Each head had
_(#)_
_____ eyes. Each alien had _____ arms and _____ legs. One of the aliens
_(#)_ _(#)_ _(#)_
was purple, the other was green. The green one said that they were from the planet Cura.

The aliens seemed friendly so _____ let the other
(teacher)
children go outside too. _____ asked how many aliens had come
(child)
on the trip. The purple creature said that there were _____ purples, _____
_(#)_ _(#)_
greens, and _____ yellows. Purples, she explained, were women, greens
_(#)_
were men, and yellows were children.

When the aliens were ready to leave, they said they could take four or five children with them for a visit to the planet Cura.

_____, and _____
(children) (child)
wanted to go, but _____ said they couldn't. So the aliens
(teacher)
decided to take _____ instead. Everyone waved good-bye.
(principal)

Name _____

# Now Try These...

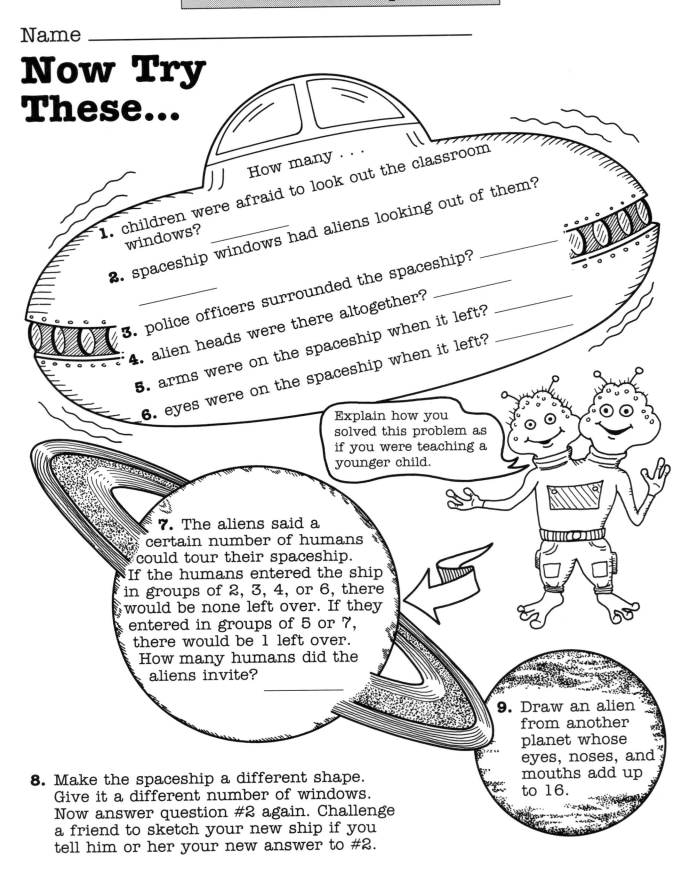

How many . . .

1. children were afraid to look out the classroom windows? _____

2. spaceship windows had aliens looking out of them? _____

3. police officers surrounded the spaceship? _____

4. alien heads were there altogether? _____

5. arms were on the spaceship when it left? _____

6. eyes were on the spaceship when it left? _____

Explain how you solved this problem as if you were teaching a younger child.

7. The aliens said a certain number of humans could tour their spaceship. If the humans entered the ship in groups of 2, 3, 4, or 6, there would be none left over. If they entered in groups of 5 or 7, there would be 1 left over. How many humans did the aliens invite? _____

9. Draw an alien from another planet whose eyes, noses, and mouths add up to 16.

8. Make the spaceship a different shape. Give it a different number of windows. Now answer question #2 again. Challenge a friend to sketch your new ship if you tell him or her your new answer to #2.

Name _____

When the class went aboard the spaceship to look around, one of the Curan children showed the class some Curan stick puzzles. Here are two of them for you to try.

**10.** Arrange, as below, 17 sticks to form 6 squares. Now, take away 5 sticks and leave 3 squares. (It may be easier to use flat toothpicks—they don't roll.)

**11.** Arrange, as below, 24 sticks to form 9 squares. Take away 8 sticks and leave 2 squares.

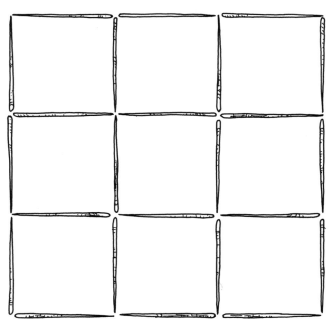

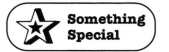 **Something Special**   Draw a floor plan of the inside of the spaceship.

# Adventure Beneath the Waves

The children of Room _____ and _____ were on their
(#)                              (teacher)

way to Florida. They had been invited by the Underwater Adventure

Company to try out a new type of scuba diving suit that had been designed

for children.

They arrived in Florida on Friday morning and then boarded a ship that

took them a short distance from shore, where the water would not be too

deep.

It didn't take long for their underwater adventure to begin. "You'll be

going down to a depth of _____ fathoms. A fathom is equal to about
(#)

6 feet," explained their guide, Dr. Watson. "Remember to check your

watches. You only have enough air in your tanks to last 1 1/2 hours." All the

children looked at their watches. It was 1:00 P.M.

After putting on the new scuba diving suits, the _____ children jumped
(#)

into the water. They jumped in groups of _____.
(#)

Six of the children saw a school of small, silvery fish. _____,
(child)

_____, and _____ each counted _____ fish.
(child)                           (child)                                          (#)

_____ counted _____ fish. _____ and
(child)                                    (#)                   (child)

_____ counted _____ each. There were so many more fish that
(child)                                    (#)

the children couldn't count them all.

Meanwhile, _____, _____, _____, and
(child)                                (child)                                (child)

_____ saw a sight they couldn't believe. It was a giant sea turtle!
(child A)

The sea turtle seemed to want to play. It allowed each child to climb aboard

its huge shell and take a ride. _____ got the longest ride, _____
                                    (child A)                              (#)
feet away and then back again. The other three children each took rides of

_____ feet and back again. They waved good-bye to the turtle as it swam off.
  (#)

   Close by, _____, and
                                (children)
_____ were carefully studying a trio of sea stars that had
        (child)
5 arms. When the sea stars moved away the children followed them to a

little cave, where they found _____ more sea stars.
                                (#)

_____, and _____
                    (children)                                  (child)
entered a large underwater cave. At first they thought the cave was empty.

Then they noticed a family of octopuses moving past them. They counted

40 arms. The children tried to follow the octopuses, but all of a sudden

they found themselves swimming in a cloud of black ink. The octopuses

disappeared.

_____, and _____
                    (children)                                  (child)
checked their watches. It was 2:20 P.M. Everyone swam back to the ship.

_____, and _____
                    (children)                                  (child)
agreed that this had been one of their best adventures.

Name _____

# Now Try These...

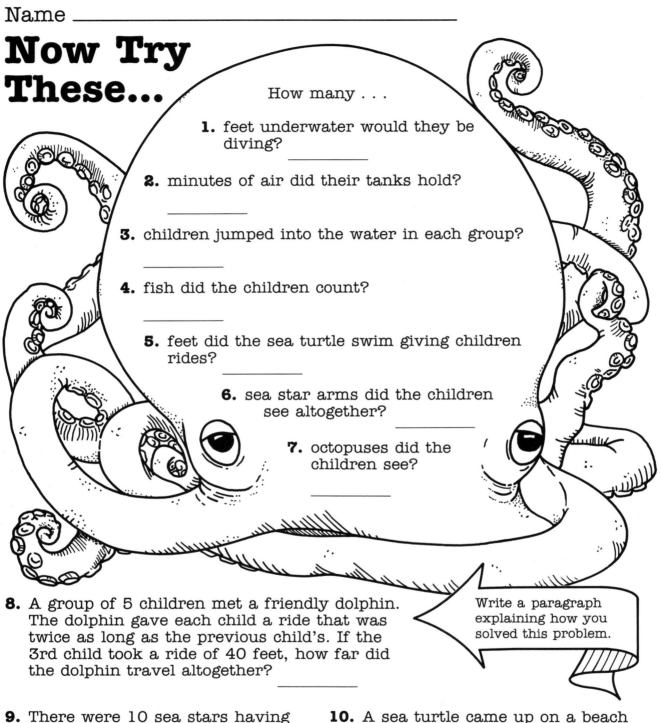

How many . . .

**1.** feet underwater would they be diving? _____

**2.** minutes of air did their tanks hold? _____

**3.** children jumped into the water in each group? _____

**4.** fish did the children count? _____

**5.** feet did the sea turtle swim giving children rides? _____

**6.** sea star arms did the children see altogether? _____

**7.** octopuses did the children see? _____

**8.** A group of 5 children met a friendly dolphin. The dolphin gave each child a ride that was twice as long as the previous child's. If the 3rd child took a ride of 40 feet, how far did the dolphin travel altogether? _____

Write a paragraph explaining how you solved this problem.

**9.** There were 10 sea stars having lunch when 4 of them suddenly <u>became</u> lunch for a bigger animal. How many arms were left at the lunch table? _____

**10.** A sea turtle came up on a beach to lay her eggs. She laid 1 egg the first minute, 3 eggs the second minute, 9 eggs the third minute, and 27 eggs the fourth minute. She continued in this way. How many eggs did she lay the fifth minute? _____

How many did she lay altogether? _____

Name _____

**11.** The answer is 60 arms.

Draw an underwater scene that includes octopuses, sea stars, humans, and anything else you would like that illustrates this answer.

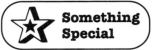 **Something Special**

What would you like to be able to do underwater? Design your own scuba diving suit that will allow you to do that.

# Missing at the Zoo

"Now remember, children, we really must stay together. The zoo is very crowded today, and it would be easy to get lost," said _____.
(teacher)

"Can we see the monkeys?" asked _____.
(child A)

"Later," said _____. "First we're going to the reptile and amphibian house."

"Snakes! Alligators! Crocodiles! Frogs! Lizards! Salamanders!" yelled

_____, and _____.
(children)        (child)

_____, and _____
(children)        (child)

stared at the huge snakes through the glass. There were _____ king cobras,
(#)

_____ boa constrictors, and _____ pythons. Each snake was 15 feet long.
(#)      (#)

_____, and _____
(children)        (child)

were looking at the frogs and toads. There were _____ frogs in each of
(#)

5 cases and _____ toads in each of 3 cases.
(#)

The children looked at exhibits of crocodiles, lizards, turtles, and salamanders. _____ and _____ counted _____ spots
(child)        (child)        (#)
altogether on the 3 spotted salamanders.

"Can we see the monkeys?" asked _____.
(child A)

"Later," said _____ "Now we're going to see the
(teacher)
nocturnal animals."

"Wow! It's really dark in here!" said _____.
(child)

"That's right," said _____. "We really have to stay
(teacher)
together in this place."

The children enjoyed looking for the nocturnal animals. They were not always easy to see in the dark exhibits.

_____, and _____
               (children)                              (child)
stared at the owls and saw _____ eyes staring back at them.
                                  (#)

_____, and _____
               (children)                              (child)
counted bats. They saw _____ bats hanging on each of _____ large branches.
                       (#)                              (#)
They estimated that _____ bats were flying around.
                      (#)

    The children blinked their eyes several times as they walked back outside into the bright sunlight. "O.K. Time for lunch," said _____.
                                     (teacher)

    They walked together to the eating area, where several small round tables were set up. There were _____ chairs and _____ tables in their section.
                           (#)               (#)

    "Where is _____?" asked _____.
                  (child A)                     (child)

    "The bathroom? The food counter? Buying a souvenir?" suggested

_____ and _____.
    (child)                   (child)
    But _____ wasn't in any of those places. Where was _____?
            (child A)                               (he/she)
_____ was becoming frantic.
    (teacher)

    "Maybe _____ is at the monkey house," said _____.
           (he/she)                                (child)
"That's where _____ kept wanting to go."
              (he/she)

_____ made the kids eat quickly. They practically ran to
    (teacher)
the monkey house. There, outside the entrance, stood _____.
                                           (child A)

    "Where have you been?" yelled _____.
                             (teacher)

    "Well, I got left behind in the nocturnal animal house. I knew you'd come to the monkey house so I figured I'd wait here. Pretty smart, huh?"

    "Well, I'm glad you're safe," said _____. "All right, class, let's go in to see the monkeys."
                                       (teacher)

    "Hey, wait a minute," said _____. "I've already been in there. I'm hungry. When do we eat?"
                               (child A)

Name _____

# Now Try These...

How many . . .

**1.** feet long were the snakes altogether? _____

**2.** frogs and toads were there? _____

**3.** spots did each salamander have? _____

**4.** owls were there? _____

**5.** bats were there? _____

**6.** chairs would there be at each table if they were divided evenly?

_____

**7.** One of the alligators at the zoo is 12 feet long. His tail is half as long as the rest of his body. How long is his tail?

_____

**8.** Two turtles are having a race. The finish line is 30 feet away.

**Turtle A** walks 3 feet per minute. She rests for 1 minute every 6 feet.

**Turtle B** walks 5 feet per minute. He rests for 3 minutes ever 10 feet.

Who wins the race? By how many minutes?

_____

What clues could you give somebody who was having trouble with #8?

Each frog in question #2 hops 3 feet. Each toad hops 4 feet. Make up a problem using this information.

Name _____

**10.** The zoo had two rules about its monkey exhibits. There could be no more than 4 howler monkeys, 5 spider monkeys, or 6 squirrel monkeys in each exhibit. And there could only be 1 species of monkey in each exhibit. The zoo had 36 of these monkeys altogether. There were the same number of howler, spider, and squirrel monkeys.

What is the fewest number of exhibits the zoo would need altogether? _____

Use the space below to design the monkey house exhibits according to the zoo's rules.

MONKEY HOUSE

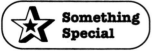
**Something Special**

A newly discovered animal has just arrived at the zoo. It protects itself in an unusual way. Draw it and give it a name. Explain how it protects itself to your friends.

# The Great Game Show Challenge

_____ and the class arrived at the television studio at
　　(teacher)

exactly 10:00 A.M. The class had been chosen to represent

_____ on the program _Sharp Kids!_, a game show on
　　(your school—school A)

which children from two different schools competed against each other. The

team that scored the most points would win prizes for the school and come

back the next week to compete against another school.

　　"I'm so nervous," said _____, as the kids from
　　　　　　　　　　　　　　　　　　　(child)

_____ came into the studio.
　　(another school—school B)

　　"They look really smart," _____ said.
　　　　　　　　　　　　　　　　　　　(child)

The announcer introduced herself and then explained how the game was

played. There would be six categories: math, science, history, geography,

literature, and health. Each category would have several questions. The team

that scored the most points would be the winner.

_____, and _____
　　　　　　(children)　　　　　　　　　　　　　　　(child)

were up first for the math questions. There were 7 questions worth 5 points

each. The questions were hard, but the children were fantastic!

_____ scored 25 points. _____
　　(school A)　　　　　　　　　　　　　　　　　　　(school B)

scored 10 points.

_____, and _____
　　　　　　(children)　　　　　　　　　　　　　　　(child)

answered the science questions. Each question was worth 7 points.

_____ scored 14 points. The other team scored 21.
　　(school A)

_____, and _____
　　　　　　(children)　　　　　　　　　　　　　　　(child)

were up for the history questions, which were worth 32 points altogether. Each team answered 2 questions correctly.

During the commercial the kids took a break.

"How are we doing?" _____ asked the teacher.
                              (child)

"You're doing fine," _____ answered.
                              (teacher)

After the commercial _____ ,
                                                (children)

and _____ were ready for the 5 geography questions.
        (child)

_____ scored 18 points. The other team scored 12 points.
      (school A)

The 6 literature questions, which were very tricky, were answered by

_____ , and _____ . The
              (children)                          (child)

questions were worth 30 points altogether. _____ got
                                                        (school A)

2 more right than their opponents.

The kids were excited. They knew they were ahead, but there was still one

category to go—health. _____ , and
                                            (children)

_____ got ready for the health questions, which were worth
   (child)

4 points each. _____ got 3 right answers, but
                       (school A)

_____ was correct 5 times.
      (school B)

There was another commercial. When it was over the announcer read

from a piece of paper in her hand. "The winning team this week is

_____ !"
   (school A)

Everyone cheered. The team from _____
                                              (school B)

congratulated the winners.

"You were super!" said their friends and family members who had been

part of the studio audience. But the children weren't really listening. They

were already thinking about winning the next week, and the week after that,

and the week after that. . . .

**53**

Name _____

# Now Try These...

How many . . .

**1.** math questions did each team answer correctly?

_____

**2.** science questions were there? _____

**3.** points was each history question worth? _____

**4.** points was each geography question worth? _____

**5.** points did each team score for literature? _____

**6.** points were all the health questions worth? _____

**7.** points did _____ win by? _____
(school A)

**8.** The class won again the next week. The children scored 3 times as many points as the other team. The total number of points scored was 180. How many points did each team score?

class _____

other team _____

**9.** During the third week's show the geography questions were worth 5 points each. The history questions were worth 4 points each. The class scored 35 points for those two topics and got 8 correct answers altogether. How many questions in each category did the class get right?

geography _____

history _____

Which of these two problems was easier for you? Explain why to a friend.

scene 2 Take 3

**10.** The answer is 52 points. Make up a problem that shows how they were scored.

Name _____

During their fourth appearance on *Sharp Kids!* the children of

_____ were behind by 13 points.
(school A)

The last category of the day was math. There would be 4 questions worth 7 points each. These are the 4 questions the children had to answer. Can you figure out each one?

**11.** How can you use five 9s to equal 100?

**12.** What two consecutive numbers have a product of 272?

**13.** Replace A, B, and C with numerals to make the equations true. What number does each letter stand for?

| | |
|---|---|
| A − C = C | A = _____ |
| A ÷ B = C | B = _____ |
| B × B = C | C = _____ |

**14.** What 2-digit number am I if the product of my digits is twice the sum of my digits?

(How many of the 4 questions would the children of _____ have to get right to win the game?) (school A)

 **Something Special**  Will there be a fifth TV appearance for the class? Write a story about what happens.

# The First Snowstorm

It was the first snowstorm of the winter. All the children were thinking about what they would do when they got home.

_____ couldn't wait to try out _____ brand-new sled.
      (child)                               (his/her)

_____ and _____ had made plans to build the world's
    (child)                       (child)
biggest snowman.

_____ was trying to teach a math lesson, but no one was
      (teacher)
listening. The children couldn't help it. Finally _____ gave up.
                                             (teacher)

_____ said, "Children, get your coats and hats. Put on your boots. We'll
(He/She)
have Snow Math."

"Did you say 'no math'?" asked _____.
                                    (child)

"I said 'Snow Math.' Hurry and get ready!"

Outside, _____ divided the _____ children into 4 groups
            (teacher)                        (#)
as evenly as possible. Then _____ gave each group a job to do.
                         (he/she)

First _____ gave directions to the children in Group One.
      (he/she)

"_____, and _____,
         (children)                       (child)
I want you to work together to make as many snowballs as you can in

1 minute." The _____ children made _____ snowballs altogether.
           (#)                 (#)

After they made the snowballs _____ told the kids they
                                      (teacher)
could divide them evenly and have a snowball fight. Everyone got really wet.

Then _____ went to the children in Group Two,
          (teacher)

_____, and _____. "I'd
         (children)                       (child A)
like each of you to make a very long footprint path. I'll give you 3 minutes to
do it."

_____ made the longest path. It had _____ footprints in it.
(child A)                                             (#)

Everyone's feet got really cold.

_____, and _____
(children)                                       (child)

were in Group Three. _____ spoke to them next. "Your job is to
(teacher)

make minisnowmen. Each snowman has to be made of 3 snowballs. See how

many snowmen you can make in 5 minutes."

After they finished the _____ minisnowmen, the kids made a giant one.
(#)

Finally _____ talked to the last group,
(teacher)

_____, and _____.
(children)                                       (child)

"Your group has to find animal tracks in the snow. Find as many as you

can."

_____ of the children found _____ bird tracks each. The rest of the group
(#)                          (#)

found _____ squirrel tracks each. But they never saw the animals that had
(#)

made the tracks.

After the children had finished their snow jobs, _____
(teacher)

let them play outside for a while. When they went back to their classroom,

_____ gave them a list of Snow Math questions.
(he/she)

"That was great!" yelled _____ when they were finished.
(child)

"Can we have Snow Science tomorrow?"

"How about Snow Spelling?" asked _____.
(child)

"We'll see," said _____ with a smile.
(teacher)

Name _____

# Now Try These...

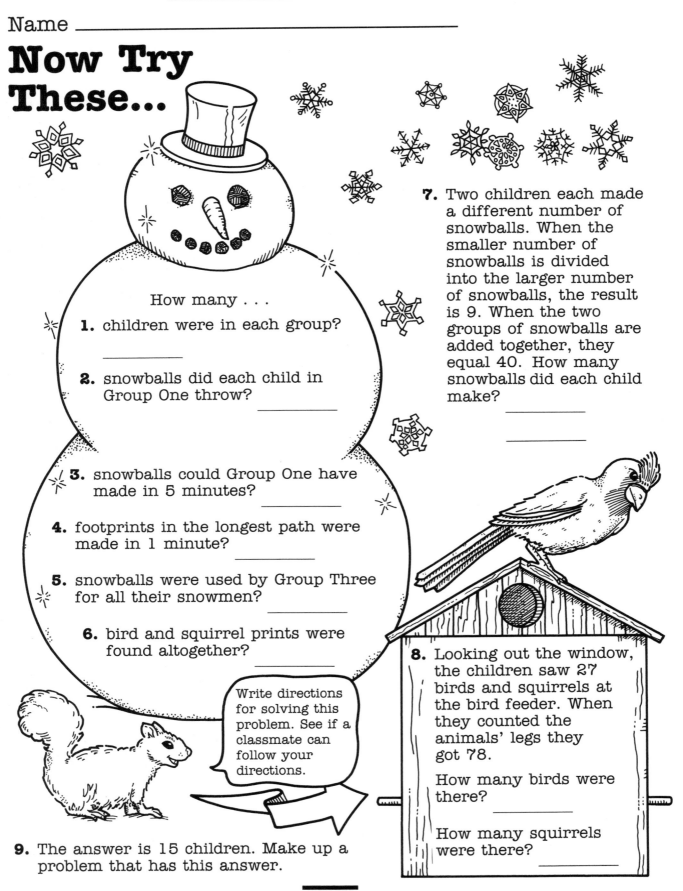

How many . . .

**1.** children were in each group?

_____

**2.** snowballs did each child in Group One throw?

_____

**3.** snowballs could Group One have made in 5 minutes?

_____

**4.** footprints in the longest path were made in 1 minute?

_____

**5.** snowballs were used by Group Three for all their snowmen?

_____

**6.** bird and squirrel prints were found altogether?

_____

Write directions for solving this problem. See if a classmate can follow your directions.

**7.** Two children each made a different number of snowballs. When the smaller number of snowballs is divided into the larger number of snowballs, the result is 9. When the two groups of snowballs are added together, they equal 40. How many snowballs did each child make?

_____

_____

**8.** Looking out the window, the children saw 27 birds and squirrels at the bird feeder. When they counted the animals' legs they got 78.

How many birds were there? _____

How many squirrels were there? _____

**9.** The answer is 15 children. Make up a problem that has this answer.

**58**

Name _____

**10.** After school that day some of the children went ice-skating. They practiced making figure eights on the ice.

Here are some eights for you to work with. Can you make these eight equations correct by putting in the missing symbols? You can use:

$$+ \quad - \quad \times \quad \div \quad ( \quad ) \quad [ \quad ]$$

**Example:** $(8\ 8+8) \div 8 = 12$

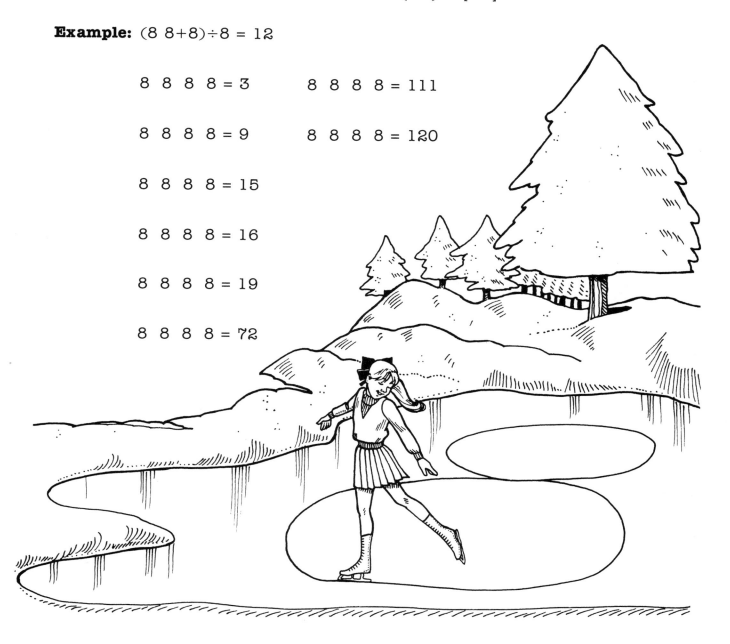

$8\ 8\ 8\ 8 = 3$          $8\ 8\ 8\ 8 = 111$

$8\ 8\ 8\ 8 = 9$          $8\ 8\ 8\ 8 = 120$

$8\ 8\ 8\ 8 = 15$

$8\ 8\ 8\ 8 = 16$

$8\ 8\ 8\ 8 = 19$

$8\ 8\ 8\ 8 = 72$

★ **Something Special**   Draw a snow scene using white chalk on black paper.

# Night Sounds

It had been a great day so far. First they set up the 6 tents. There were

_____ children, five parents, and the teacher, so there would be one adult
(#)

and several children in each tent.

Then most of the kids went fishing. _____, _____,
(child)                    (child)

_____, and _____ each caught _____ fish.
(child)                (child)                   (#)

_____, and _____ each
(children)                              (child)

caught _____. _____ and _____ caught _____ each.
(#)            (child)                (child)                  (#)

They figured out how many fish they would need for dinner and threw the

rest back into the water.

Dinner was delicious. Then the kids settled down to toast marshmallows.

Each child had _____ marshmallows. The adults only had _____ each.
(#)                                        (#)

_____, and _____
(children)                              (child)

took turns telling ghost stories. Everyone shivered.

By midnight everyone was asleep except _____. _____ kept
(child A)              (He/She)

hearing sounds. First it was the hooting of owls. Then _____ heard a
(he/she)

rustling noise in the bushes. _____ shook _____.
(He/She)           (child B)

"Hey, why did you wake me?" _____ asked.
(child B)

"Do you hear that sound?" whispered _____.
(child A)

"What do you think it is?" asked _____.
(child B)

"I don't know. Maybe a snake."

_____ woke up. "What's going on?" _____ asked.
(child C)                                  (He/She)

"We hear noises," whispered _____ "We think it's a snake."
(child B)

_____ listened. "Maybe it's a bear!"
(child C)

Now they were really scared. Finally they picked up their flashlights and slowly unzipped the tent flap. At first they didn't see anything. Then they heard the noises again, louder this time and closer! Nervously, the three children shone their flashlights in the direction of the sound and laughed at what they saw—two raccoons in search of a free meal! When the light shone on them the two raccoons scurried away.

"I was really scared for a few minutes," said _____.
(child A)

"So was I," agreed _____.
(child B)

The next morning the three children decided not to tell anyone about their midnight adventure.

The class had another wonderful day. _____, _____,
(child)          (child)
_____, _____, and _____ went swimming.
(child)          (child)          (child)
Each one swam _____ times across the small lake.
(#)
_____, and _____
(children)                              (child)
went berry picking in the woods. They completely filled their bucket. Later when they counted up their berries, they found they had _____. They divided
(#)
them equally.

That night _____, _____, and _____
(child A)          (child B)          (child C)
slept soundly, but the next morning all the other children were talking about the sounds in the night.

"I heard a snake!" yelled _____.
(child)

"I heard a bear!" exclaimed _____.
(child)

_____, _____, and _____ just smiled.
(child A)          (child B)          (child C)

Name _____

# Now Try These...

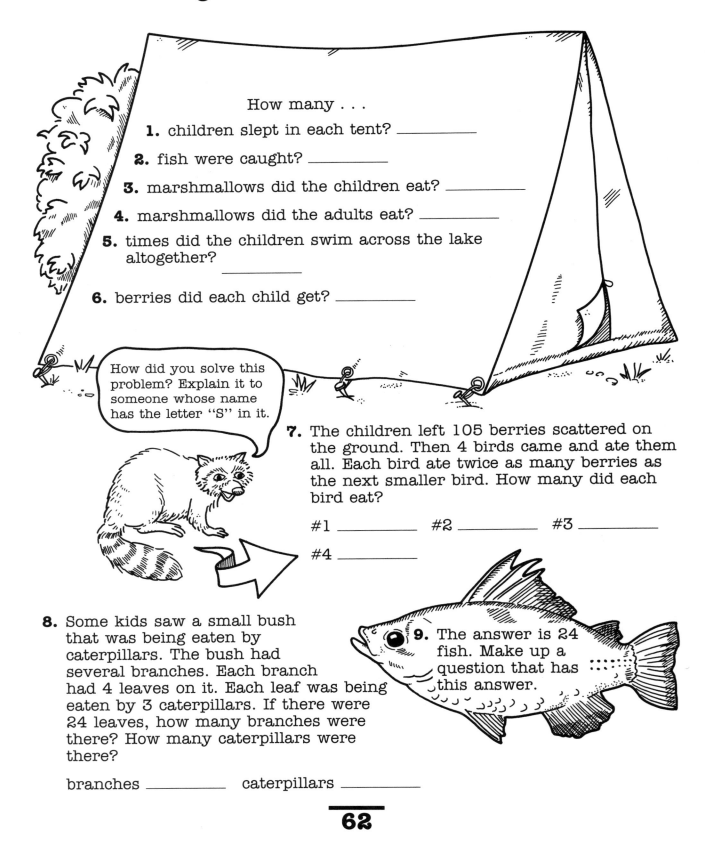

How many . . .

1. children slept in each tent? _____

2. fish were caught? _____

3. marshmallows did the children eat? _____

4. marshmallows did the adults eat? _____

5. times did the children swim across the lake altogether? _____

6. berries did each child get? _____

How did you solve this problem? Explain it to someone whose name has the letter "S" in it.

7. The children left 105 berries scattered on the ground. Then 4 birds came and ate them all. Each bird ate twice as many berries as the next smaller bird. How many did each bird eat?

#1 _____ #2 _____ #3 _____

#4 _____

8. Some kids saw a small bush that was being eaten by caterpillars. The bush had several branches. Each branch had 4 leaves on it. Each leaf was being eaten by 3 caterpillars. If there were 24 leaves, how many branches were there? How many caterpillars were there?

branches _____ caterpillars _____

9. The answer is 24 fish. Make up a question that has this answer.

**62**

Name _____

**10.** Replace the letters with numbers to make true equations. The same letters within a puzzle stand for the same numbers.

$$
\begin{array}{r}
H\ O\ O\ T \\
+\ H\ O\ O\ T \\
\hline
O\ W\ L\ S
\end{array}
$$

$$
\begin{array}{r}
D\ A\ R\ K \\
\times\ \ \ \ \ N \\
\hline
S\ C\ A\ R\ Y
\end{array}
$$

 **Something Special**

When the children shone their flashlights in the direction of the sounds, they didn't see raccoons. Draw what they saw.

# Super Stars

The _____ children of Room _____ were very excited. They were going to
   (#)                        (#)

be in a movie called *Super-Teach*, about a teacher who was really a robot.

Today was the day that filming would begin.

At 9:15 A.M. the classroom door opened. _____ walked in,
                                              (principal)

followed by the person who would play the robot, then the movie director,

the camera crew, and a lot of other people.

The robot was just like a regular teacher, but _____ would be
                                                 (he/she)

superstrong, superfast, and supersmart.

In the first scene, _____, and
                                  (children)

_____ were supposed to be doing a project about the Knights
   (child)

of the Round Table. Super-Teach used their building set to build a castle.

_____ used all 560 blocks in 4 minutes.
(He/She)

Scene Two was very exciting—the class pencil sharpener broke.

_____, and _____ tried
              (children)                        (child)

to fix it but couldn't. Super-Teach sharpened _____ pencils for each child in
                                                 (#)

the class, with _____ teeth!
                 (his/her)

Scene Three took place at recess. Super-Teach played catch with

_____, and _____.
              (children)                        (child)

_____ threw the ball to the kids _____ times altogether.
(He/She)                                (#)

Then Super-Teach played basketball with _____,
                                              (child)

_____, _____, and _____. Each child had
    (child)           (child)               (child)

_____ chances to shoot the ball. Super-Teach had _____ chances. _____
 (#)                                               (#)              (He/She)

made all _____ shots. The kids made half of theirs.
          (his/her)

In Scene Four Super-Teach read a _____-page book to the class. _____
(#)                                                              (He/She)
finished it in _____ minutes. _____ spoke so quickly that
                 (#)            (He/She)

_____, and _____
                    (children)                        (child)
couldn't understand a word _____ said.
                            (he/she)

In the last scene the bus broke down and Super-Teach had to take

_____, and _____ home.
                    (children)                        (child)
The trip to take each child home took _____ seconds.
                                        (#)

When the filming was over for the day, the director told the children that
they had done a great job. Their part in the movie was over. The rest of the
scenes would be shot in different places.

The kids said good-bye to Super-Teach and the rest of the crew.

"Do you think they'll ask us to be in *Super-Teach II*?" asked

_____.
      (child)
"Of course," said _____. "We're Super Stars!"
                        (child)

**65**

Name _____

# Now Try These...

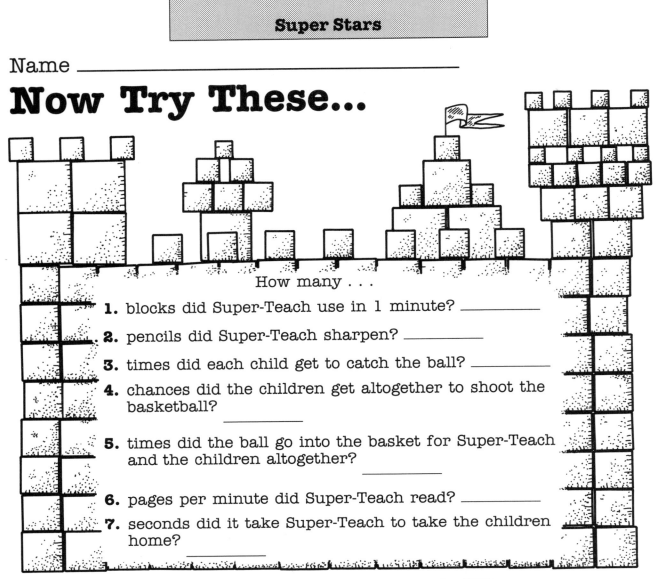

How many . . .

1. blocks did Super-Teach use in 1 minute? _____

2. pencils did Super-Teach sharpen? _____

3. times did each child get to catch the ball? _____

4. chances did the children get altogether to shoot the basketball? _____

5. times did the ball go into the basket for Super-Teach and the children altogether? _____

6. pages per minute did Super-Teach read? _____

7. seconds did it take Super-Teach to take the children home? _____

"Since you're such smart kids," said Super-Teach, "I'll leave you with some really tough problems to solve."

"Here's the first one."

8. Rearrange the numbers 4324 into a number that can be evenly divided by 7. _____

"This is the second one."

9. Make this a true equation by using multiplication and addition signs.

    9   8   7   6   5   4   3   2   1   0 = 100

"Here's the third problem."

10. How many triangles do you see? _____

Can you think of a plan that will help you count the triangles?

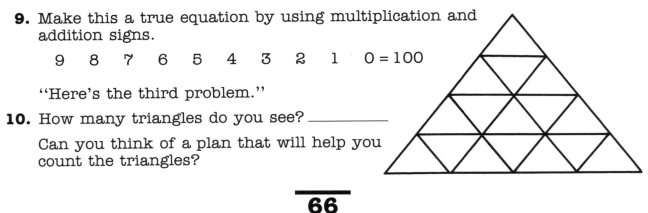

Name _____

"Here's the last one," said Super-Teach, "just for you Super Stars!"

**11.** Use the numbers 1 to 12 (except for 7 and 11) so that each line of the star equals 24.

**Make it easier!** Write the numbers on small squares of paper. Move them around on the star until you get the right answer.

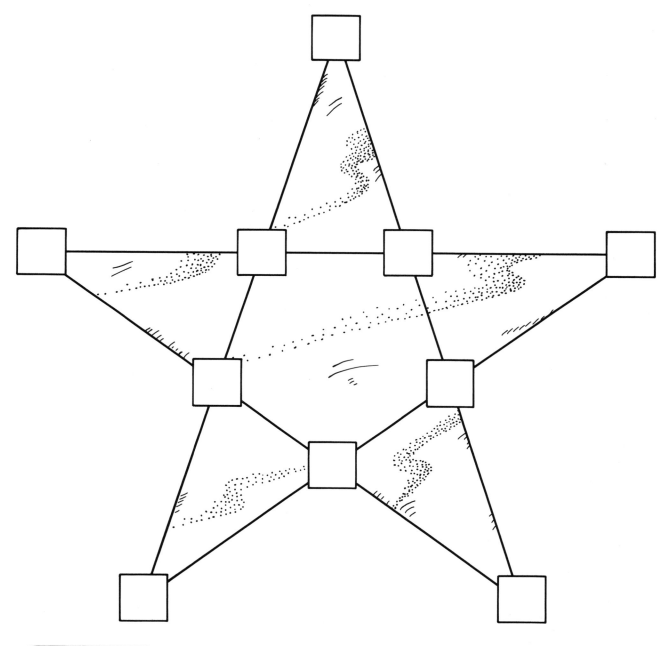

 **Something Special** Super-Teach was a robot. What do you think Super-Teach looked like inside? Draw your ideas.

# The Missing Wallet

The _____ children were lined up at the entrance to the aquarium.
       (#)

_____ paid for their tickets. It cost $1.25 for each child to
        (teacher)

get in. _____ had to pay $2.50 for _____.
              (teacher)                                    (himself/herself)

The children were interested in all the fish, but the shark exhibit was

their favorite. _____ and _____ got as close to the shark
                   (child A)                 (child)

tank as they could. "Boy, they sure look mean," said _____.
                                                            (child A)

_____, and _____
              (children)                      (child)

looked for the shy little octopus in his tank. But all they could see was one

long arm snaking out of a cave.

_____, and _____
              (children)                      (child)

liked the fish from the tropical reef. They loved the bright colors of the clown

fish and the butterfly fish.

There was a special exhibit where you could touch living sea creatures.

_____, and _____ picked
              (children)                      (child)

up a horseshoe crab. They were amazed to find out that horseshoe crabs had

been around in the days of the dinosaurs.

_____, and _____
              (children)                      (child)

picked up snails and sea stars, oysters, and clams.

The morning went by quickly. It was time for lunch and then a trip to

the gift shop. Each child had brought 50 cents for a drink and $1.00 for

souvenirs. _____ was holding their money.
                  (teacher)

The kids sat down at the lunch counter while _____ and
                                                    (child)

_____ went to buy the drinks. After lunch they went to the gift shop.
        (teacher)

**68**

"Remember, you each have $1.00 to spend," said _____ (teacher) as they went in the door.

_____ (child B) picked out fish stickers for 45 cents and an octopus pencil sharpener for a quarter.

_____ (child C) chose 2 shells that cost 20 cents each and a whale book for 50 cents.

_____ (child D) wanted 2 plastic sharks for 27 cents each, a dolphin pencil for 19 cents, and a penguin eraser for 15 cents.

_____ (child) spent all _____ (his/her) money on 4 sea animal postcards.

Finally everyone had chosen souvenirs. The children lined up at the cash register. _____ (teacher) reached for _____ (his/her) wallet to give the children their dollars. The wallet was gone!

They looked all around the gift shop, but the wallet wasn't there. They retraced their steps through the aquarium. They went back past the touch tank, the tropical fish tank, the octopus, the sharks—all the way back to the entrance of the aquarium where they had paid for their tickets, but they couldn't find the wallet. They checked at the Lost and Found, but no one had turned in the wallet.

"Wait a minute," _____ (child) said. "Didn't you have the wallet when you paid for our drinks?"

The whole class and the teacher ran back to the lunch counter. When the cashier saw them _____ (he/she) smiled and held up the wallet. They thanked _____ (him/her) and raced back to the gift shop.

"Boy, am I glad we got our money back," said _____ (child B). "These stickers are really cool!"

Name _____

# Now Try These...

How much . . .

1. did the aquarium tickets cost altogether? _____

2. did the all drinks cost? _____

3. did _____ spend?
   (child B)

4. did _____ spend?
   (child C)

5. did _____ spend?
   (child D)

6. did each animal postcard cost? _____

7. What coins could
   _____ ,
   (child B)
   _____ , and
   (child C)
   _____ have
   (child D)
   received in change?

8. You have $1.00 to spend at the aquarium, but you must follow these rules:

   a. Spend exactly $1.00.
   b. Buy four items.
   c. Do not buy more than two of the same thing.

   Use the items and prices from the story.

ONE BIG ONE

9. On the way home the teacher asked three children how much change they had.

   ■ The first child said, "I have 1 coin."
   ■ The second child said, "I have 2 coins."
   ■ The third child said, "I have 3 coins."

   No one had more than 50 cents in change. How much money could each child have?

How many possibilities can you find for each child?

Name _____

**10.** Arrange 10 pennies like this:

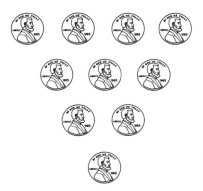

Move only 3 pennies to make them look like this:

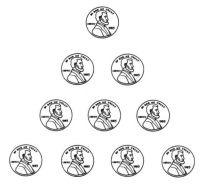

---

**11.** Arrange 6 pennies so that there are 2 rows of 4 coins each. (There are two ways to do this.)

---

**12.** Arrange 3 pennies so that the end coins are tails up and the center coin is heads up.

You must make *three* moves, turning over 2 coins at a time to make them look like this:

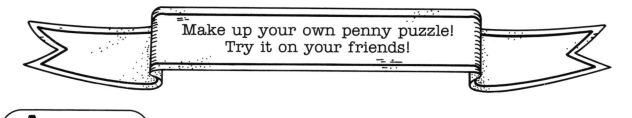

---

Make up your own penny puzzle!
Try it on your friends!

 **Something Special**

Design an aquarium exhibit for your favorite sea creature.

# Bus Breakdown

It had been an exhausting day at the zoo. The children had had a great time, but they were glad to be getting on the bus. When the driver dropped them off at 9:30 that morning, _____ said to meet _____ at 2:00 P.M. for
$\quad\quad\quad$ (he/she) $\quad\quad\quad$ (him/her)
the trip home.

"There's the bus!" yelled _____ and _____.
$\quad\quad\quad\quad\quad$ (child) $\quad\quad\quad\quad\quad$ (child)

"Right on time," said _____.
$\quad\quad\quad\quad\quad$ (child)

They boarded the bus quickly, fastened their seat belts, and were ready for the 45-minute trip back to school.

On the way home the kids talked about their fun day at the zoo.

_____, and _____ liked
$\quad\quad\quad$ (children) $\quad\quad\quad\quad$ (child)

the monkeys best. _____, and
$\quad\quad\quad\quad\quad\quad$ (children)

_____ thought the snakes were great.
$\quad$ (child)

They had been traveling for 15 minutes when the bus started making funny noises. The driver pulled over to the side of the road and stopped the bus.

"Something's wrong," said the driver. "I'll have to go and call the bus company so they can send another bus."

"Please ask them to hurry. We're supposed to be back at school before

3:00 P.M.," said _____.
$\quad\quad\quad\quad\quad$ (teacher)

_____, and _____
$\quad\quad\quad$ (children) $\quad\quad\quad\quad$ (child)

were worried. They had to be at soccer practice at 3:15 P.M. They might be late.

_____, and _____
$\quad\quad\quad$ (children) $\quad\quad\quad\quad$ (child)

were upset. They were supposed to be at a birthday party at 3:30 P.M. They might be late.

_____, and _____
         (children)                                     (child)
were playing at a friend's house that afternoon. They were being picked up at 3:00 P.M. They might be late.

_____ had a piano lesson at 3:15 P.M. _____ might be late.
      (child A)                                       (He/She)
_____ hoped so.
(He/She)

The bus driver returned 15 minutes later. _____ did not look happy.
                                                    (He/She)

"All the large buses are being used now. It will take an hour for one to pick us up. But," the driver continued, "the company can send us one minibus. It can be here in 10 minutes."

"Would we all fit in one minibus?" _____ asked.
                                                (teacher)

"No. It would take half the children back to school and then come back here for the rest."

"Well," said _____, "I think we'll just have to wait for
                           (teacher)
the large bus. I don't want to split the class up."

The bus driver smiled. "I thought you would say that so I told the company to send the large bus."

An hour was a long time to wait. _____,
                                                       (children)
and _____ played tic-tac-toe.
      (child)

_____, and _____
         (children)                                     (child)
counted red cars as they went by.

The bus arrived on time. A half hour after that the children were back at school.

Everyone was glad to be home, especially _____, who had
                                                  (child A)
missed _____ piano lesson.
      (his/her)

Name _____

# Now Try These...

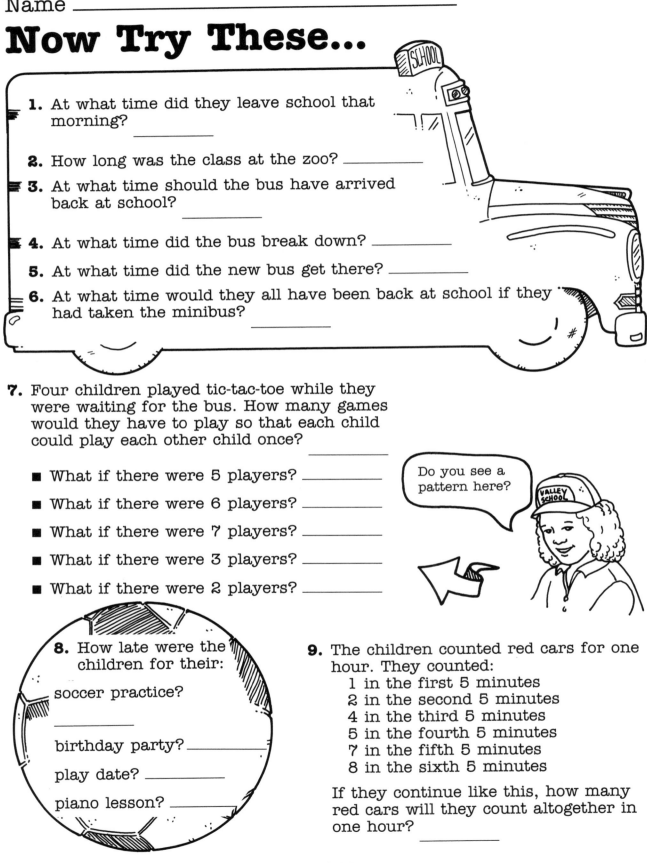

1. At what time did they leave school that morning? _____

2. How long was the class at the zoo? _____

3. At what time should the bus have arrived back at school? _____

4. At what time did the bus break down? _____

5. At what time did the new bus get there? _____

6. At what time would they all have been back at school if they had taken the minibus? _____

7. Four children played tic-tac-toe while they were waiting for the bus. How many games would they have to play so that each child could play each other child once? _____

   ■ What if there were 5 players? _____

   ■ What if there were 6 players? _____

   ■ What if there were 7 players? _____

   ■ What if there were 3 players? _____

   ■ What if there were 2 players? _____

   Do you see a pattern here?

8. How late were the children for their:

   soccer practice?

   _____

   birthday party? _____

   play date? _____

   piano lesson? _____

9. The children counted red cars for one hour. They counted:
   1 in the first 5 minutes
   2 in the second 5 minutes
   4 in the third 5 minutes
   5 in the fourth 5 minutes
   7 in the fifth 5 minutes
   8 in the sixth 5 minutes

   If they continue like this, how many red cars will they count altogether in one hour? _____

Name _____

**10.** Make up a schedule for a trip to the zoo. Spend four hours there. Be sure that your schedule answers the following questions:

■ At what time will you arrive?

■ What animals will you see? At what time will you see them?

■ How long will you have for lunch?

■ Will you buy souvenirs? How much time do you need for that?

■ Do you need time to walk from one animal area to another?

■ At what time will the bus pick you up to go home?

Write your schedule below.

---

# Zoo Schedule

_____    _____

_____    _____

_____    _____

_____    _____

_____    _____

_____    _____

_____    _____

_____    _____

_____    _____

_____    _____

_____    _____

---

 **Something Special**   Invent a new game that you can play while waiting for something. Write down the rules.

# The Bake Sale

The children had read in the newspaper that the animal shelter in

_____ was in trouble. There were so many homeless cats
(name of town)

and dogs that the shelter was running out of room and food for them all.

The children discussed the problem at lunch.

"I wish we could help them," said _____.
(child)

"We could adopt some animals," _____ said.
(child)

"We could collect animal food," suggested _____.
(child)

"I know!" _____ exclaimed. "Let's think of a way to earn
(child)

money that we can give to the shelter."

"Good idea!" said _____. "Maybe we could sell something. Any
(child)

ideas?"

"How about a bake sale?" suggested _____. "We could sell
(child)

cake, cookies, cupcakes, and stuff like that."

Everyone liked the idea.

After lunch they discussed it with _____. _____ liked
(teacher)          (He/She)

the idea also.

That night the kids told their parents about the sale. The parents said

they would help with the baking.

Finally it was the day of the sale. The children hoped they would earn a

lot of money for the animal shelter.

_____, and _____
(children)                        (child)

sold happy face cookies. The faces were made of M&Ms. They sold _____
(#)

cookies for _____ cents each.
(#)

_____, and _____
　　　　　　　　　　　　　(children)　　　　　　　　　　　　　　　　　　　　　(child)

sold ___ cupcakes with creamy pink filling. The cupcakes cost ___ cents each.
　　　(#)　　　　　　　　　　　　　　　　　　　　　　　　　　　　　　　　(#)

_____, and _____
　　　　　　　　　　　　　(children)　　　　　　　　　　　　　　　　　　　　　(child)

sold popcorn balls. The popcorn was all different colors. _____ people bought
　　　　　　　　　　　　　　　　　　　　　　　　　　　　　　　　　(#)

them for _____ cents each.
　　　　　　(#)

_____, and _____
　　　　　　　　　　　　　(children)　　　　　　　　　　　　　　　　　　　　　(child)

were selling cookies shaped like dogs and cats. The dog cookies were bigger

so they cost _____ cents. _____ were sold. The cat cookies only cost _____
　　　　　　　(#)　　　　　　(#)　　　　　　　　　　　　　　　　　　　　　　(#)

cents. _____ of those were sold.
　　　　(#)

_____, and _____
　　　　　　　　　　　　　(children)　　　　　　　　　　　　　　　　　　　　　(child)

were selling slices of chocolate cake for _____ cents each. They sold the
　　　　　　　　　　　　　　　　　　　　　　　　(#)

whole cake, _____ slices.
　　　　　　　(#)

_____ and _____ sold star-shaped cookies for
　　　　(child)　　　　　　　　　　　(child)

_____ cents. For an extra _____ cents they would write your name with
　(#)　　　　　　　　　　　　(#)

chocolate frosting. They sold _____ plain cookies and _____ with names.
　　　　　　　　　　　　　　　(#)　　　　　　　　　　　　　(#)

　　The bake sale was over at 2:00 P.M. because everything had been sold.

The children counted the money. After school _____ took
　　　　　　　　　　　　　　　　　　　　　　　　　　　　　(teacher)

the money to the animal shelter.

　　A few days later the class received a letter from the animal shelter. The

letter thanked the children for sending the money. It also said that because

of the newspaper story many animals had been adopted, including three by

children from _____.
　　　　　　　　　(school)

_____ smiled. "I'm one of the kids who adopted a dog. Guess
　　　(child)

what we named her? Cookie!"

**77**

Name _____

# Now Try These...

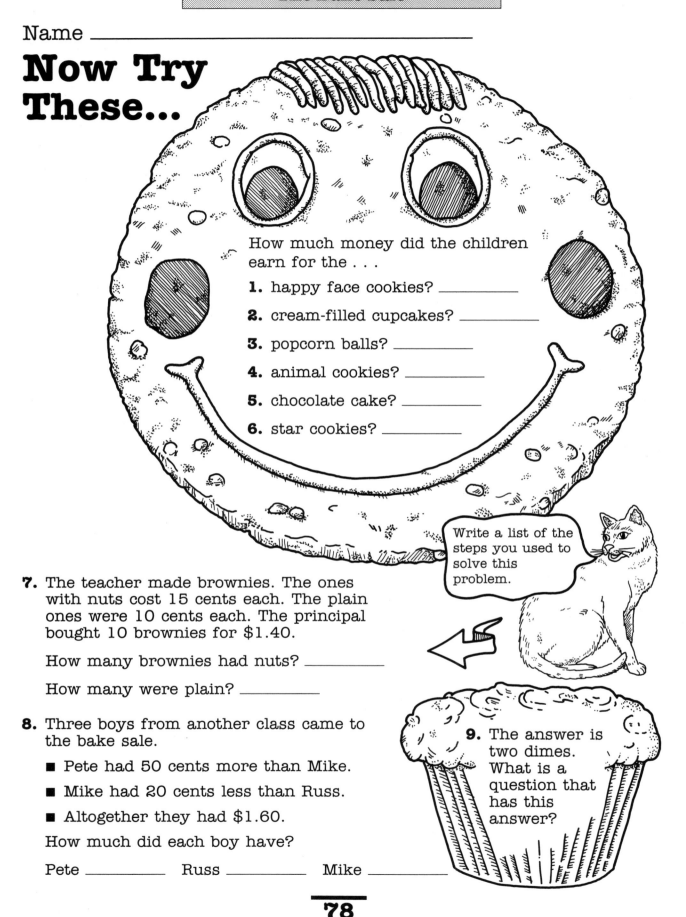

How much money did the children earn for the . . .

1. happy face cookies? _____
2. cream-filled cupcakes? _____
3. popcorn balls? _____
4. animal cookies? _____
5. chocolate cake? _____
6. star cookies? _____

Write a list of the steps you used to solve this problem.

7. The teacher made brownies. The ones with nuts cost 15 cents each. The plain ones were 10 cents each. The principal bought 10 brownies for $1.40.

   How many brownies had nuts? _____

   How many were plain? _____

8. Three boys from another class came to the bake sale.

   ■ Pete had 50 cents more than Mike.

   ■ Mike had 20 cents less than Russ.

   ■ Altogether they had $1.60.

   How much did each boy have?

   Pete _____ Russ _____ Mike _____

9. The answer is two dimes. What is a question that has this answer?

Name _____

**10.** Emily, a fourth grade girl, bought something for 50 cents at the bake sale. Could she have paid the 50 cents, exactly, using the following coins?

| Number of coins | What coins could be used? |
| --- | --- |
| 1 coin? | |
| 2 coins? | |
| 3 coins? | |
| 4 coins? | |
| 5 coins? | |
| 6 coins? | |
| 7 coins? | |
| 8 coins? | |
| 9 coins? | |
| 10 coins? | |

**Something Special** What ingredients would you use for the world's most delicious cake? Write the recipe.

# Surprise!

The children of Room _____ wanted to have a surprise party for
(#)

_____. They decided that they would all try to find jobs to
(teacher)

earn some money for the party. They could work after school and on

weekends.

First they divided themselves into teams. Each team would work for

50 cents an hour. Then they gave themselves a name—Kids-4-Hire.

_____ and _____ made up advertising notices and
(child)              (child)

asked the other kids at school to take the notices home. Lots of people called.

They all needed hard workers.

_____, and _____
(children)                              (child)

worked in a neighbor's yard pulling weeds from 1:30 P.M. to 4:00 P.M. They

were really hot when they finished.

_____, and _____
(children)                              (child)

worked at the supermarket. They helped carry groceries to people's cars.

Their team earned $2.00. They were really hungry when they finished.

_____, and _____
(children)                              (child)

baby-sat for a set of five-year-old twins. They started at 3:00 P.M. and earned

$1.75. They were really tired when they finished.

_____, and _____
(children)                              (child)

helped a storekeeper fix up her shelves. They worked from 3:15 P.M. to

5:15 P.M. for 3 days. They were such good workers that the storekeeper

gave them an extra dollar. They were really happy when they finished.

_____, and _____
(children)                              (child)

helped a woman clean her house. They started working at 8:10 A.M. and ended at 12:40 P.M. They were really dirty when they finished.

_____ and _____ collected and counted all the
(child)                    (child)
money.

_____ and _____ made a list of the things they
(child)                    (child)
would need for the party.

_____ and _____ went shopping for the food and
(child)                    (child)
decorations.

While _____ was at lunch the following day,
(teacher)

_____ and _____ set everything up for the party.
(child)                    (child)

When _____ walked into the room after lunch, the
(teacher)

children were all hiding. When _____ turned on the lights everyone yelled,
(he/she)

"Surprise!"

_____ was really surprised. At the end of the party
(teacher)

_____ said, "This is the best party I've ever had in my whole life. I'll
(he/she)

never forget it!"

Name _____

# Now Try These...

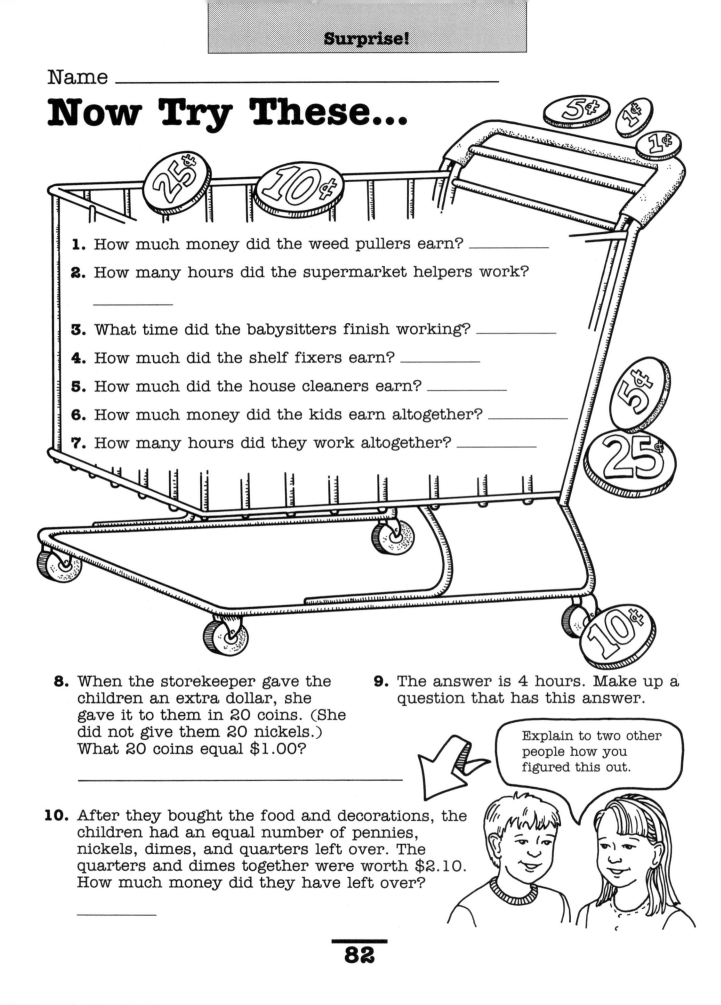

1. How much money did the weed pullers earn? _____

2. How many hours did the supermarket helpers work?

   _____

3. What time did the babysitters finish working? _____

4. How much did the shelf fixers earn? _____

5. How much did the house cleaners earn? _____

6. How much money did the kids earn altogether? _____

7. How many hours did they work altogether? _____

8. When the storekeeper gave the children an extra dollar, she gave it to them in 20 coins. (She did not give them 20 nickels.) What 20 coins equal $1.00?

   _____

9. The answer is 4 hours. Make up a question that has this answer.

   Explain to two other people how you figured this out.

10. After they bought the food and decorations, the children had an equal number of pennies, nickels, dimes, and quarters left over. The quarters and dimes together were worth $2.10. How much money did they have left over?

   _____

Name _____

**11.** The children bought the party things (ice cream, cake, paper plates, and balloons) at four different stores (Ellen's Emporium, Stanley's Shop, Patrick's Place, and Marian's Mart).

At which store did they buy each item?

**Clue 1.** Ellen's Emporium and the store that sells cake are next door to each other.

**Clue 2.** Stanley's Shop doesn't sell food.

**Clue 3.** Patrick's Place and the store that sells plates are across the street from Ellen's Emporium.

**Clue 4.** Marion buys balloons from the store next door.

|  | Ellen's Emporium | Stanley's Shop | Patrick's Place | Marian's Mart |
|---|---|---|---|---|
| ice cream |  |  |  |  |
| cake |  |  |  |  |
| paper plates |  |  |  |  |
| balloons |  |  |  |  |

 **Something Special**

Think of a party with a theme (outer space, book characters, etc.). Plan food, decorations, and entertainment to go with that theme. Write down your ideas.

# Future Park (Part 1)

"This is going to be the greatest thing we've done all year," said

_____.
    (child)

"That's for sure!" _____ yelled happily.
                   (child)

It was the grand opening of Future Park. Just before the gates opened

_____ said, "Remember, we are meeting at the Space
    (teacher)

Shuttle ride at 11:45 A.M. Have fun!"

_____, and _____
             (children)                        (child A)

headed straight for the Galaxy Special, the world's fastest, highest, longest

roller coaster. It cost _____ cents a ride.
                   (#)

"Awesome!" said _____ when it ended.
                   (child A)

The others agreed, so they went on again.

Another group—_____, and
                        (children)

_____—went into the Monster Maze. It was a gigantic maze that
    (child)

was really hard to find your way through. It cost _____ cents to get in.
                                            (#)

Getting out was free, but it wasn't easy.

There were 5 kids who paid 3 quarters, 8 dimes, and 4 nickels altogether

to go through a door that said "Feet First." Inside, _____ put on
                                                 (child)

a pair of high-top sneakers and found _____ playing
                                     (himself/herself)

basketball with Michael Jordan—and winning!

_____ slipped on a pair of ballet shoes and became the star of
    (child)

Swan Lake.

_____ put on a pair of ruby red shoes and found
    (child)

_____ in Oz.
(himself/herself)

_____ laced up a pair of ice skates and won a speed skating
　　(child)

race at the Olympics.

_____ pulled on a pair of swimming flippers and explored a
　　(child)

sunken ship.

"Wow!" said all five when they got out.

Some of the kids were hungry. They stopped at the Rainbow Cotton Candy

stand. There were 16 different colors to choose from, and each color had a

different flavor. The price was 5 cents a color.

_____ had _____ colors. _____ had _____ colors.
　　(child)　　　　　　(#)　　　　　　　　　(child)　　　　　　(#)

_____ , and _____ had
　　　　　　(children)　　　　　　　　　　　　　　　　　(child)

_____ colors each.
(#)

"Delicious," they all agreed.

_____ , and _____
　　　　　　(children)　　　　　　　　　　　　　　　　(child)

paid _____ dimes and _____ nickels each to go on a great adventure. On a
　　(#)　　　　　　(#)

ride called Journey, you could put on a special helmet, think of a special

place, and instantly it would seem like you were there! The children decided

to share the same journey and went to Antarctica.

"Incredible!" said _____ when they returned. They wanted to
　　　　　　　　　(child)

go on a second journey, but another group—_____ ,
　　　　　　　　　　　　　　　　　　　　　　　(children)

and _____—was waiting for a turn.
　　(child)

At 11:45 A.M. everyone met _____ at the Space Shuttle ride.
　　　　　　　　　　　　　(teacher)

This was supposed to be the best ride in the park! The kids couldn't wait.

TO BE CONTINUED

Name _____

# Now Try These...

How much . . .

1. did the group spend to ride the Galaxy Special? _____

2. did the group pay to go through the Monster Maze? _____

3. did each child pay for Feet First? _____

4. was spent on Rainbow Cotton Candy? _____

5. did the group spend to go to Antarctica? _____

6. more did the most-expensive ride cost than the least-expensive ride? _____

7. The children found an incredible candy counter at the park. The first child spent 5 cents. The second child spent 10 cents. The third child spent 15 cents, and so on, with each child spending 5 cents more than the child before. If $2.25 was spent altogether, how many children bought candy?

_____

Explain to a classmate how you got the answer.

8. Five children paid 35 cents each to ride the Superhigh Ferris Wheel. They each paid using different coins. How did they pay? Compare answers with a friend. Did you have the same answers? Can you find more ways to pay?

9. Make up a problem that has these ingredients:

■ four children
■ $2.50
■ two rides

Give your problem to a friend to solve.

Name _____

**10.** One of the children said, "I don't have very much money left." She wouldn't say how much money she had, but she gave four clues. Can you use the clues to figure out how much money the girl had left?

**Make it easier!** Use Clue #1 to make a list of the possible amounts.

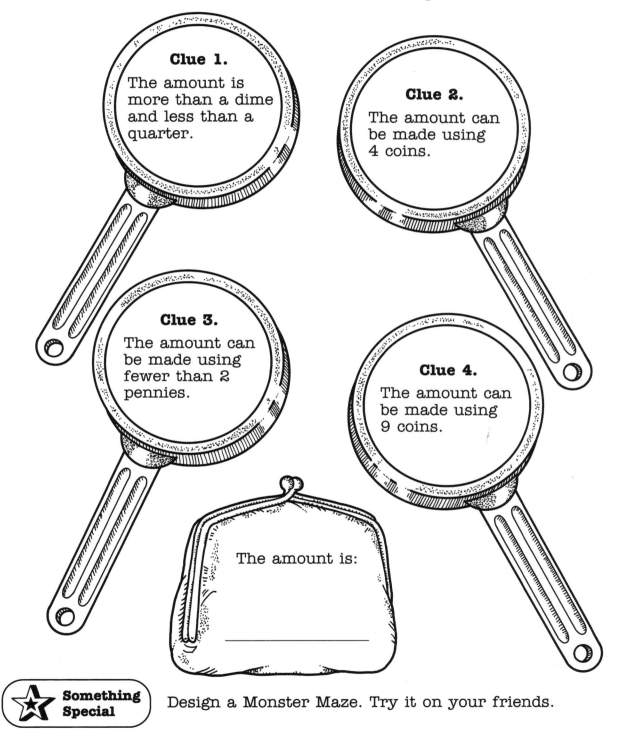

**Clue 1.**
The amount is more than a dime and less than a quarter.

**Clue 2.**
The amount can be made using 4 coins.

**Clue 3.**
The amount can be made using fewer than 2 pennies.

**Clue 4.**
The amount can be made using 9 coins.

The amount is:

_____

**Something Special**   Design a Monster Maze. Try it on your friends.

# Future Park (Part 2)

As soon as the shuttle hatch opened, the children started running up the ramp. _____ (children) , and _____ (child) were the first ones on board the Space Shuttle ride. The rest of the class and _____ (teacher) quickly followed.

The children heard a voice coming from a speaker above them: "This is Mission Control. Please fasten your seat belts. Liftoff will be in one minute."

_____ (child) looked at the shuttle clock. It was exactly 12:00 P.M. The voice from Mission Control continued, "10, 9, 8, 7, 6, 5, 4, 3, 2, 1, liftoff."

"It really feels like we're moving!" _____ (child) yelled over the roar of the shuttle's engines. It *did* feel like they were zooming into space.

_____ (children) , and _____ (child) closed their eyes. So did everyone else.

_____ (child) looked at the clock. It had been 15 minutes since liftoff. Then _____ (he/she) looked out the window. "Wow, what a ride! It looks like we're in outer space." Everyone looked. It *did* seem like outer space—dark!

A half hour later Mission Control said, "We are now in orbit. You can move around the cabin." _____ (child) , _____ (child) , _____ (child) , and _____ (child) unbuckled their seat belts and immediately floated into the air. _____ (teacher) looked astonished.

"That can't happen unless there's no gravity! But that's impossible. This is just a ride. Isn't it?"

After 20 minutes Mission Control came on again. "Lunch is now ready. The trays are in the oven to your right."

_____ , and _____ had
(children)                                          (child)

hot dogs. Everyone else had hamburgers. For dessert there was freeze-dried

ice cream, chocolate and vanilla. _____ didn't eat.
                                                          (teacher)

They finished lunch at 1:30 P.M. _____ , _____ , and
                                                          (child)                        (child)

_____ found several space suits. They decided to try them on.
(child)

It took 20 minutes to get into the suits and a half hour to get out of them

again. The whole class laughed. But _____ didn't.
                                                              (teacher)

Then _____ , and
            (children)

_____ discovered an exercise treadmill. Everyone wanted to try
(child)

it. There were 8 kids who exercised for 5 minutes each before Mission

Control came on again. "Please return to your seats and prepare for

landing." _____ looked worried.
                    (teacher)

Finally the voice of Mission Control was heard again. "Touchdown." The kids

cheered. _____ took one last look at the shuttle clock. It was 3:30 P.M.
                  (child)

The hatch opened. Then everyone ran down the ramp.

_____ blinked. The sun was still high in the sky. Something
(teacher)

was wrong! At 3:30 P.M. the sun should be much lower. _____ looked at
                                                                                        (He/She)

_____ watch—12:15 P.M.! Some of the children were looking at their
(his/her)

watches in amazement.

_____ and the children looked at each other and laughed.
(teacher)

"Wow!" they yelled. "What a ride!"

**89**

Name _____

# Now Try These...

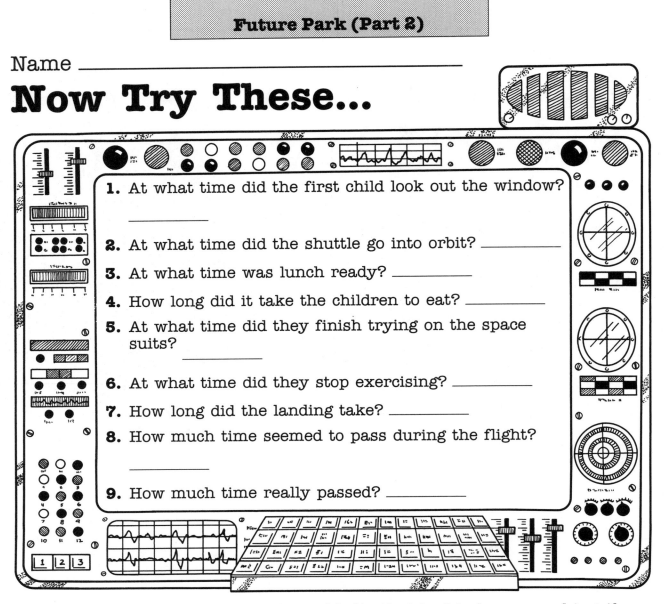

1. At what time did the first child look out the window?

    _____

2. At what time did the shuttle go into orbit? _____

3. At what time was lunch ready? _____

4. How long did it take the children to eat? _____

5. At what time did they finish trying on the space suits?

    _____

6. At what time did they stop exercising? _____

7. How long did the landing take? _____

8. How much time seemed to pass during the flight?

    _____

9. How much time really passed? _____

10. Two children found some nuts and bolts that had to be screwed together. It wasn't easy to do in zero gravity, but they did their best. The first child put together 2 nuts and bolts each minute. The second child put together 3 sets each minute. If they work together, how many minutes will it take them to screw together 75 nuts and bolts? _____

Can you do this more than one way?

11. Take the numbers 1–12 off the clock. Can you divide those numbers into two equal groups that have the same sum?

2  11  5  8

1  12  4

6  3  9

7

10

Name _____

**12.** Here is the time schedule for a real shuttle launch.

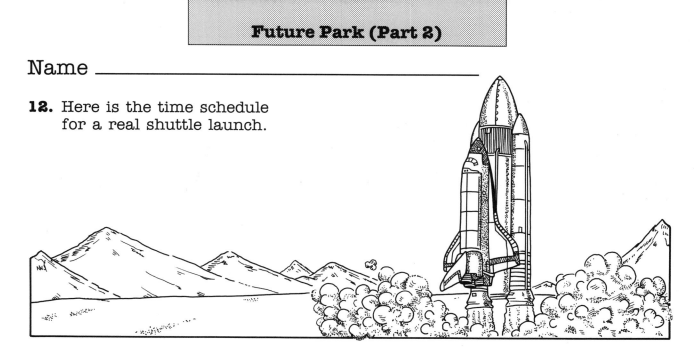

| TIME | EVENT |
|---|---|
| 3:00 A.M. | Begin final countdown. |
| 6:10 A.M. | Astronauts enter orbiter. |
| 6:50 A.M. | Check communications with Mission Control. |
| 6:55 A.M. | Ground crew closes side hatch. |
| 7:30 A.M. | Ground crew leaves shuttle area. |
| 7:40 A.M. | Load flight plan into computer. |
| 7:54 A.M. | Check all switches. |
| 7:59 A.M. | Start power units and engines. |
| 8:00 A.M. | LIFTOFF |
| 8:02 A.M. | Solid Rocket Booster separates from orbiter. |
| 8:09 A.M. | External Tank separates from orbiter. |
| 8:46 A.M. | Orbit is achieved. |

Make up your own questions based on this schedule. Ask your classmates to solve the problems.

 **Something Special**   Design your own Future Park ride or design another theme park (for example: Western World, Dinosaur Days, Folktale Village, etc.).

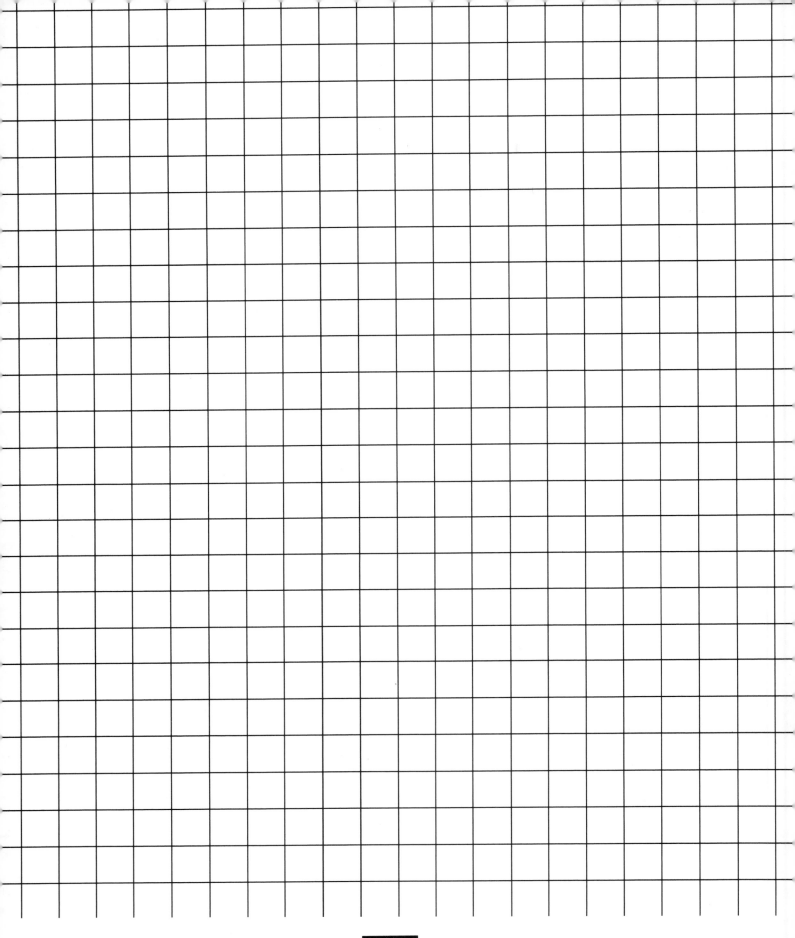

# Answer Key

## The House on Haunted Hill (pp. 10-11)

**9.** 8 minutes (When he reaches the 10th step he is at the top and doesn't slip back.)

**10.** 17 cups

**12.**
```
    5       8
      3   6
        7
        1   2
    4       9
```

## Back to the Past (Part 1) (p. 14)

**2.** 120 seconds

**7.** Any of the following:
4 triceratops, 0 iguanodons
3 triceratops, 2 iguanodons
2 triceratops, 4 iguanodons
1 triceratops, 6 iguanodons
0 triceratops, 8 iguanodons

**8.** Six ways: 139, 193, 319, 391, 913, 931

## Back to the Past (Part 2) (pp. 18-19)

**6.** 18 feet tall

**7.**

**8.** 40 small dinosaur prints

**10.** The year is 1903.

1907, 1908, 1909, 1916, 1917, 1918, and 1919 are wrong because of Clue #3.

1902, 1904, 1906, 1911, 1913, and 1915 are wrong because of Clue #4.

1901 and 1910 are wrong because of Clue #5.

1905 and 1914 are wrong because of Clue #6.

1912 is wrong because of Clue #7.

## Batter Up! (pp. 22-23)

**8.** 46 bags of peanuts
21 bags of popcorn

**9.**

| innings | | |
|---|---|---|
| 1st | 2nd | 3rd |
| 4 | 0 | 0 |
| 0 | 4 | 0 |
| 0 | 0 | 4 |
| 3 | 1 | 0 |
| 3 | 0 | 1 |
| 0 | 3 | 1 |
| 1 | 3 | 0 |
| 0 | 1 | 3 |
| 1 | 0 | 3 |
| 2 | 2 | 0 |
| 2 | 0 | 2 |
| 0 | 2 | 2 |
| 2 | 1 | 1 |
| 1 | 2 | 1 |
| 1 | 1 | 2 |

**11.** Angels 10, Rangers 8
Red Sox 9, Orioles 3
Tigers 7, Indians 1
Brewers 5, Yankees 2
Mariners 3, Blue Jays 1
White Sox 4, Twins 2
Royals 5, A's 1

## Treasure Hunt (p. 26)

**1.** 8 + 6 + 4 = 18 meters

**2.** 12 + 24 = 36 meters

**3.** 40 − 13 = 27 meters

**4.** (24 + 50) − 60 = 14 meters

**5.** 22 meters

**6.** 95 meters

## Lost in the Woods (pp. 30-31)

**7.** 26 branches

**8.** 18

**10.** The 12 pentominoes are:

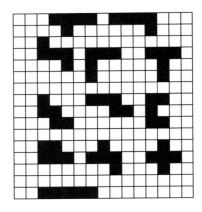

## Gerbil Trouble (pp. 34-35)

**7.** ninth day

**8.**
| | |
|---|---|
| guinea pig | 10:00 A.M. |
| gerbil | 1:00 P.M. |
| hamster | 3:00 P.M. |

**10.**

| Word | Chart 1 | Chart 2 |
|---|---|---|
| rat | 39 | 42 |
| mouse | 73 | 62 |
| hamster | 84 | 105 |
| beaver | 53 | 109 |
| muskrat | 103 | 86 |
| squirrel | 119 | 97 |
| chipmunk | 95 | 121 |
| woodchuck | 103 | 140 |
| guinea pig | 89 | 154 |

## Planetarium Puzzle (pp. 38-39)

**1.** 31 stars

**2.** 12 stars

**3.** Big Dipper and Leo

**5.** 14 hours

**7.** 33 stars

**8.** 32 marbles

**10.**

| Planet | Moons |
|---|---|
| Mercury | 0 |
| Venus | 0 |
| Earth | 1 |
| Mars | 2 |
| Jupiter | 16 |
| Saturn | 18 |
| Uranus | 15 |
| Neptune | 8 |
| Pluto | 1 |

## Visitors from Space (pp. 42-43)

**7.** 36 humans

**10.**  **11.**

## Adventure Beneath the Waves (p. 46)

**2.** 90 minutes

**7.** 5 octopuses

**8.** 310 feet

**9.** 30 arms

**10.** 81 eggs in the fifth minute
121 eggs altogether

## Missing at the Zoo (pp. 50-51)

**7.** 4 feet long

**8.** Turtle B wins by 2 minutes.

**10.** 3 howler monkey exhibits
3 spider monkey exhibits
2 squirrel monkey exhibits
8 exhibits altogether

## The Great Game Show Challenge (pp. 54-55)

**1.** 5 questions, 2 questions

**2.** 5 questions

**3.** 8 points

**4.** 6 points

**5.** 20 points, 10 points

**6.** 32 points

**7.** 16 points

**8.** 135 points, 45 points

**9.** 3 geography questions
5 history questions

**11.** $[(99 \times 9) + 9] \div 9 = 100$

**12.** $16 \times 17 = 272$

**13.** A = 8, B = 2, C = 4

**14.** 36 or 63
(The class needed to answer at least 3 questions correctly in order to win.)

## The First Snowstorm (pp. 58-59)

**7.** 4 snowballs, 36 snowballs

**8.** 15 birds, 12 squirrels

**10.** $(88 \div 8) - 8 = 3$
$[(8 \times 8) + 8] \div 8 = 9$
$(8 + 8) - (8 \div 8) = 15$
$[(8 \div 8) \times 8] + 8 = 16$
$8 + (88 \div 8) = 19$
$88 - (8 + 8) = 72$
$888 \div 8 = 111$
$[(8 + 8) \times 8] - 8 = 120$

## Night Sounds (pp. 62-63)

**7.** 7, 14, 28, and 56 berries

**8.** 6 branches
72 caterpillars

**10.**

| HOOT | 2,553 |
|---|---|
| +HOOT | +2,553 |
| OWLS | 5,106 |

| DARK | 8,497 |
|---|---|
| ×N | ×3 |
| SCARY | 25,491 |

(There are other possibilities.)

## Super Stars (pp. 66-67)

**1.** 140 blocks

**8.** 2443

**9.** $9 \times 8 + 7 + 6 + 5 + 4 + 3 + 2 + 1 + 0 = 100$

**10.** 27 triangles
(16 made of 1 triangle
7 made of 4 triangles
3 made of 9 triangles
1 made of 16 triangles)

**11.**

```
        6
      2 /\ 5
  9 <       > 8
      4    3

     12    10
```

## The Missing Wallet (pp. 70-71)

**3.** 70 cents      **5.** 88 cents

**4.** 90 cents      **6.** 25 cents

**7.** 30 cents = 1 quarter
1 nickel, etc.
10 cents = 1 dime, etc.
12 cents = 2 nickels
2 pennies, etc.
(There are many other possibilities.)

**8.** Whale book, shell, two penguin erasers. (Several other combinations are possible.)

**9.** Child 1: 1, 5, 10, 25, or 50 cents
Child 2: 2, 6, 10, 11, 15, 20, 26, 30, 35 or 50 cents
Child 3: 3, 7, 11, 12, 15, 16, 20, 21, 25, 27, 30, 31, 35, 36, 40, or 45 cents

**10.**          **11.**

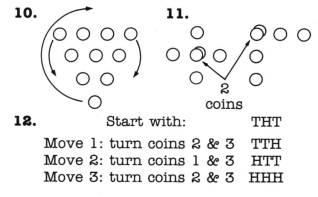

coins

**12.**          Start with:          THT
Move 1: turn coins 2 & 3      TTH
Move 2: turn coins 1 & 3      HTT
Move 3: turn coins 2 & 3      HHH

## Bus Breakdown (p. 74)

**1.** 8:45 A.M.      **3.** 2:45 P.M.

**2.** $4\frac{1}{2}$ hours      **4.** 2:15 P.M.

**5.** 3:30 P.M.     **6.** 4:10 P.M.

**7.** 4 players: 6 games
5 players: 10 games
6 players: 15 games
7 players: 21 games
3 players: 3 games
2 players: 1 game

**8.** soccer practice    45 minutes
birthday party    30 minutes
play date    60 minutes
piano lesson    45 minutes

**9.** 108 cars

## The Bake Sale (pp. 78-79)

**7.** 8 brownies with nuts
2 plain brownies

**8.** Pete: 80 cents
Russ: 50 cents
Mike: 30 cents

**10.**  1 coin:  half dollar
2 coins: 2 quarters
3 coins: no
4 coins: 1 quarter, 2 dimes, 1 nickel
5 coins: 5 dimes
6 coins: 1 quarter, 5 nickels
7 coins: 3 dimes, 4 nickels
8 coins: 1 quarter, 2 dimes,
5 pennies
9 coins: 1 dime, 8 nickels
10 coins: 10 nickels
(Other answers are possible.)

## Surprise! (pp. 82-83)

**1.** $1.25          **3.** 6:30 P.M.

**2.** 4 hours        **4.** $4.00

**5.** $2.25

**6.** $10.25 + $1.00 = $11.25

**7.** $20\frac{1}{2}$ hours

**8.** 1 quarter, 4 dimes, 5 nickels,
10 pennies

**10.** $2.46 (6 of each coin)

**11.** ice cream       Patrick's Place
cake            Marian's Mart
paper plates    Stanley's Shop
balloons        Ellen's Emporium

**Reasoning:**

**Clue #1**  Since Ellen's is next door to the cake store, it is not the cake store.

**Clue #2**  Since Stanley's does not sell food, it is not the ice cream or cake store.

**Clue #3**  Neither Patrick's nor Ellen's sells plates. Since Patrick's Place is not next door to Ellen's, it does not sell cake (see Clue #1). Therefore Marian's sells cake (and is next door to Ellen's). Stanley's is the only one left to sell plates.

**Clue #4**  Marian's is next to Ellen's, so Ellen's sells balloons. Patrick's must sell ice cream.

## Future Park (Part 1) (pp. 86-87)

**3.** 35 cents

**7.** 9 children

**8.** 3 dimes, 1 nickel
7 nickels
1 quarter, 1 dime
1 quarter, 2 nickels
35 pennies
(There are many other possible combinations.)

**10.** 21 cents

11, 14, 15, 18, 19, 23, and 24 cents are wrong because of Clue #2.

12, 13, 17, and 22 cents are wrong because of Clue #3.

16 and 20 cents are wrong because of Clue #4.

## Future Park (Part 2) (p. 90)

**1.** 12:15 P.M.      **4.** 25 minutes

**2.** 12:45 A.M.      **5.** 2:20 P.M.

**3.** 1:05 P.M.       **6.** 3:00 P.M.

**7.** 30 minutes

**8.** 3 hours 30 minutes

**9.** 15 minutes     **10.** 15 minutes

**11.** 1, 2, 3, 10, 11, 12 = 39
4, 5, 6, 7, 8, 9     = 39
(There are other combinations.)